WITHDRAWN
D0171697

Local Radio Journalism

WITHDRAWN

Local Radio Journalism

Paul Chantler
and
Sim Harris

FOCAL PRESS

Focal Press
An imprint of Butterworth-Heinemann Ltd
Linacre House, Jordan Hill, Oxford OX2 8DP

PART OF REED INTERNATIONAL BOOKS

OXFORD LONDON BOSTON
MUNICH NEW DELHI SINGAPORE SYDNEY
TOKYO TORONTO WELLINGTON

First published 1992

© Butterworth-Heinemann 1992

All rights reserved. No part of this publication may be reproduced in any material form (including photocopying or storing in any medium by electronic means and whether or not transiently or incidentally to some other use of this publication) without the written permission of the copyright holder except in accordance with the provisions of the Copyright, Designs and Patents Act 1988 or under the terms of a licence issued by the Copyright Licensing Agency Ltd, 90 Tottenham Court Road, London, England W1P 9HE. Applications for the copyright holder's written permission to reproduce any part of this publication should be addressed to the publishers

British Library Cataloguing in Publication Data
Chantler, Paul
Local Radio Journalism
I. Title II. Harris, Sim
070.4

ISBN 0 240 51308 8

Library of Congress Cataloguing in Publication Data
Chantler, Paul.
Local radio journalism/Paul Chantler and Sim Harris.
p. cm.
Includes index.
ISBN 0 240 51308 8
1. Radio journalism – United States. 2. Journalism, Regional – United States. I. Harris, Sim, 1946– . II. Title.
PN1991.3.U6C47
070.1'94–dc20 92–24650
CIP

Composition by Genesis Typesetting, Laser Quay, Rochester, Kent
Printed and bound in Great Britain by Redwood Press, Melksham, Wiltshire

Contents

Foreword

Between now and the end of the century, The Radio Authority intends to license up to three hundred new local radio stations. Although under the provisions of the new Broadcasting Act none of these will be required to provide what is known as 'public service' programmes, many of them will undoubtedly include news, local information and a certain amount of current affairs in their programme schedules.

This book is intended as a practical guide and handbook for anyone who wants to acquire the skills necessary for success in local radio journalism – and indeed for practising radio journalists who want to develop and extend their skills. It is a happy circumstance that such a book should appear at this important stage in the development of radio in this country.

Radio journalism is a highly specialized craft. There are no pictures – moving or still – to help to tell the story. The images have to be created in the mind of the listener entirely through the medium of sound. Yet the power and appeal of radio is such that the skilled radio journalist can often tell a more vivid story than his colleagues and competitors in television or newspapers.

On the other hand, as the authors make clear in their book, there are certain principles common to responsible journalism in any medium. Accuracy, objectivity and the careful distinction between fact and opinion are the hallmarks of serious professional journalism; and a proper regard for personal privacy and the sensitivities of other people mark the difference between the responsible reporter and the sensation-mongering hack

The authors underline these important matters in the context of the real world of local radio, and of the journalist working with limited resources in a small, computerized newsroom.

As Group Programme Director and Head of News for the Chiltern Radio Network, with many years of local radio journalism behind him, Paul Chantler is well qualified to provide expert guidance for anyone setting up a news operation for a local, incremental or community radio station. Sim Harris, too, is very experienced in both Independent and BBC Radio and takes a particular interest in training.

This book will be a useful addition to the bookshelf of any newsroom, however small.

Lord Chalfont, Chairman, The Radio Authority

Preface

When television became popular, in the 1950s, there were predictions that radio would die. Forty years on, radio is actually much more exciting and diverse than ever before. It offers a challenging career to journalists at all levels, from the well-resourced and established network newsrooms to the small operations in community radio, sometimes staffed by a single person.

This book is a working manual for radio journalists. Maybe you are trying to set up a new station, or are looking for your first job with an existing one. Maybe you have worked in radio for some time. We hope that whatever your experience, you find this book helpful.

In the legal section, although we have done our best to emphasize the main points in the space available, we do recommend McNae's *Essential Law For Journalists* as a much fuller guide. It is by Tom Welsh and Walter Greenwood, published by Butterworths. A newsroom is on dangerous ground without an up-to-date copy.

Like any industry, radio journalism has its own jargon. Rather than litter the text with repetitive explanations which some readers will not need, we have included a Glossary. Turn to it if you are in doubt.

We would like to thank the people who helped with our research and made many valuable suggestions. We are also grateful to the radio stations, both BBC and Independent, who kindly allowed us to take photographs on their premises, and to Sara Cavan for her photographs of GLR.

Finally, if any errors remain, they are our responsibility alone. We would be glad to hear about them, for the benefit of readers of future editions.

Paul Chantler
Sim Harris

Acknowledgements

We are particularly grateful to the following people and organizations who have helped in the preparation of the text and illustrations for this book:

Lord Chalfont, Chairman, The Radio Authority; Colin Mason, Richard Robinson, Mike Vince, Sheila Mallett, Bill Overton and Geoff Cutmore at the Chiltern Radio Network; Paul Robinson at BBC Radio One; Matthew Bannister of the BBC; Tony Talmage and Steve Brodie at BBC Wiltshire Sound; Tony Attwater and Roger Holdom at Beacon Radio/WABC; Marantz Hi-Fi UK Ltd; John Perkins at Independent Radio News; and Gill Robinson for preparing the manuscript.

1

The structure of British local radio

Local radio in Britain started in 1967 when the BBC opened Radio Leicester as an experiment. Before that, there had been regional programmes but not truly local stations.

The BBC retained its monopoly for six years, until the first commercial Independent Radio (IR) station, LBC, opened in London in 1973. It was followed a few days later by Capital Radio. The launch of IR and BBC Radio One was largely the result of the popularity of music-based pirates like Radio Caroline, relying on transmitters outside the UK.

The years of development

Both networks grew in the following years. By mid-1992, there were 43 BBC and 90 IR stations.

The BBC naturally controlled its own network, whereas the Independent Broadcasting Authority was responsible for the commercial stations. The IBA selected the contractors, owned the transmitters and laid down standards for programming, advertising and engineering. In practice, the IBA Technical Code of Practice made building new stations expensive because of the strict controls it imposed on technical equipment and the soundproofing of studios. Programming standards were also rigorously enforced; for example, an IR station could not change the duration of its news bulletins without IBA approval.

A 'lighter touch'

Today the situation has changed. The Radio Authority took over from the IBA in January 1991 with the intention of governing local radio with a 'lighter touch'. This means less rigorous controls, allowing stations to develop more individual styles of output and widen listener choice.

The 1980s

The original IR network consisted of fairly large stations mainly covering substantial areas of the country. A large catchment area was essential to generate enough income from advertising. In one case, expenditure exceeded revenue so disastrously that the station concerned went off the air. The IBA was anxious to avoid a repetition and, although several other stations have come dangerously close to collapse, strategic mergers and rescue packages have ensured that this episode has remained unique.

As the 1980s proceeded, it became clear that expansion of the IR network was being hampered by the high costs involved. Many areas, including much of Wales and Scotland, remained without commercial radio.

Community radio

Meanwhile a number of highly vocal community radio groups had failed to convince the government that smaller stations would be viable until the late 1980s. As part of a general review of broadcasting, small 'incremental' stations were finally permitted. They were established alongside existing large IR stations and – in the words of the former IBA – they are 'incremental' to an existing service, i.e. they provide a second, more localized service in the same area. They are less tightly controlled than earlier IR companies, but their revenues are much smaller; it remains to be seen whether they are all viable.

Today's network

The British local radio network therefore works on several levels today. The BBC local network, unaffected by advertising revenue, covers most of the country, including the more remote areas. It has a brief to provide at least 70% speech programmes and is given resources and staff to match.

The commercial network can be divided into three groups. The first consists of the 'traditional' IR stations which obtained their franchises before 1987. Such stations were allocated at least two frequencies, one on AM and the other on FM.

The second group is smaller. The catchment area of these stations is about the same as those in the first group but they only have one frequency, usually on FM. It should be added that all IR stations in the first group are becoming obliged to provide 'split' programme services on AM and FM if they want to keep both frequencies.

The third group is the most varied, consisting of a growing number of small 'community' stations. The Radio Authority plans to oversee the development of these smaller stations during the next decade.

2

So you want to be on the radio?

Understanding radio

Research shows that many people think the sheer brevity of radio news means it is the purest source of news available.

They perceive newspaper news as lagging behind radio and TV. The downmarket tabloids are seen simply as titillating scandal sheets featuring more on TV and film stars than real news events; the broadsheets are more concerned with analysis and comment. Television too is a complex medium needing a great many people to make it work, with its ability to react fast to a news story sometimes hampered by technicalities.

People listen to radio news when they need to know what is going on quickly. They realize that because radio news is so short, it has to concentrate simply on reporting the facts.

Speed and simplicity

Radio is probably at its best when it is 'live' or reacting to an event happening 'now'. Because there are relatively few technicalities, a news story can be on the air in seconds and updated as it develops. Radio works best with news stories which require a quick reaction. There is a flexibility which exists in no other media because comparatively few people are involved.

Radio can simply be one person, a tape recorder and a telephone. There are no cameras, lights or production assistants.

Usually it is just one broadcaster and a microphone separating him or her from the listener. You should always strive to make use of radio's greatest assets – speed and simplicity.

Making pictures

Radio is the best medium to stimulate the imagination. The listener is always trying to imagine what he hears and what is being described. These pictures are emotional – such as the voice of a mother appealing for information about her missing teenage daughter. Pictures on radio are not limited by the size of a screen. They are any size you wish.

Person-to-person

Radio is a very personal medium. The broadcaster is usually speaking directly to the listener. This is why it is so important to think of the audience as singular. When you talk on the radio, you are not broadcasting to the masses through a gigantic public address system, you are talking to *one* person in the way you would speak if you were holding a conversation over a cup of coffee or a pint of beer.

Radio also allows the full emotions of the human voice to be heard, from laughter to anger and pain to compassion. The sound of a voice can convey far more than reported speech. This is because the way something is said is just as important as what is being said.

How local is local?

The biggest strength of broadcasting news on local radio is that it gives the station a sense of being truly local. Radio stations aiming for a broad audience ignore news at their peril. In an increasingly competitive marketplace, news is one of the few things which makes a local station sound distinctive.

News from around the corner is often just as important as news from around the world, if not more so in many cases. There is a danger in becoming too local though. Policy judgements often have to be made about what is local and what is parochial or parish pump. For instance, a story about a cat up a tree is too parochial for almost all radio stations. The same story about a firefighter being killed while trying to rescue the cat is not only a good local story, it is almost certainly a national one as well.

What makes a good broadcaster?

Working in radio is a very public job. We all have a good chance to hear how it is done whether we prefer Radio One, Radio Three, the nearest Independent Local Radio station or the BBC World Service.

But what qualities are managers seeking in their staff?

It is essential that you should know what you want to do. The first letters to be rejected by radio stations start: 'I would be willing to do anything, including making the tea . . .'. The writers of such letters believe they are increasing their chances by showing versatility. In fact, people who are too dazzled by radio in general are unlikely to be much use in practice.

Apart from journalists, the other major on-air performers are the presenters (or 'announcers' in parts of the BBC). That can cover all kinds of broadcasting, from being a disc jockey on a fast-moving pop music show to reading the shipping forecast on Radio Four.

The qualities of a radio journalist

There has rarely been a better time to start in radio. The industry is growing fast and the main problem facing editors is finding sufficient staff who can do the job. Note the words 'who can do the job'. There is no shortage of people who would like to do it. Sadly not all of them have abilities to match their ambition.

A competent radio journalist has to combine the traditional talents of the reporter with the newer skills of broadcasting. Traditional talents mean an ability to write clear, easily understood English, a knack of summarizing complicated situations and – most difficult of all – a 'nose for news' or knowing what makes a good story.

The radio journalist must feel at home with technical equipment. This means editing tape, dubbing audio, recording links and packages, reading news live on air and conducting interviews. If all those words mean nothing, do not worry. They are all explained in the Glossary.

The good radio journalist is flexible, able to deal with a major disaster and a funny story in the same hour or two, and also imaginative. That does not mean making stories up, but seeing newsworthy possibilities in unpromising places, like apparently endless council meeting minutes. Journalists must be able to think on their feet, perhaps recording an interview or writing a court case literally five minutes before it is due on air.

Starting out

There are some journalists in broadcasting who are never heard on the radio. They may be sub-editors working in a big national newsroom like the BBC General News Service or Independent

Figure 2.1 The modern newsroom at Independent Radio News (Courtesy of Derek Rowe).

Radio News (Figure 2.1). But such people are usually highly experienced. Their jobs are rarely offered to newcomers.

The novice journalist starting out in radio is more likely to find a job at a local station and that means a smaller newsroom where everyone has to have a go at everything. The news editor might well take part in newsreading and reporting and, during part of the day, the news staff may be reduced to just one person. Weekend shifts, if they happen at all, are frequently handled by one person doing everything from presenting bulletins to making hourly check calls and grabbing an interview or two between times.

There is one phrase that should never be heard in a small radio newsroom – 'that isn't my job'. The versatility of a radio journalist is most fully stretched at local stations. In dozens of small newsrooms, there are no specialists concentrating on just one type of subject like Industry or Politics, there are no sub-editors and there may not even be a newsroom secretary.

Today's news is very often presented by journalists. The old style news 'reader' still survives on BBC national radio and on the World Service. Under the traditional system, the newsreader provides the voice and the news is written by other people. On local radio, the bulletins are presented by the reporting staff.

There is one more quality we have not yet mentioned – at least not specifically. That quality is *enthusiasm*.

Make no mistake, the job can be hard. It may mean unpredictably long hours when a big story breaks. It may be demanding, with split-second deadlines to meet every day. It may even be lonely as you keep a newsroom going on a boring Sunday afternoon. It will certainly be unsocial – someone has to work Christmas Day! But it can also be very enjoyable as you get back with the lead story just in time or present a 'hard' bulletin, full of good, breaking stories. In other words, the job can be great fun and highly satisfying. It is what you make it.

How to get a job

There is no traditional route into radio journalism. It is highly competitive and persistence is essential. Although it is desirable to have a high level of education, it is by no means a necessity. However, some organizations recruit virtually all graduates. Others prefer experience over education.

The best advice for young people wanting to become radio journalists is to combine the highest level of education with as much work experience as possible. Many newsrooms welcome work experience students as an extra pair of hands, and although you may find yourself doing menial tasks such as tape reclaiming, it is an invaluable opportunity to observe how the news machine works.

Local newspapers

Experience of working on a local newspaper is still one of the best ways to get a job in local radio, although the writing techniques are different. People from local papers come to radio with a thorough grounding in the rudiments of journalism.

They are trained in law, public administration, typing and shorthand – all useful skills for the radio journalist. They also have experience in covering all sorts of stories ranging from flower shows to inquests. Accuracy and balance are second nature to these people, who also tend to know the difference between a police sergeant and a superintendent! Papers are also the best way to have developed that essential 'nose' for news.

Hospital radio

In the way that local papers provide a grounding in journalism, hospital radio stations give a good grounding in practical radio skills. It is voluntary work, with a chance to try everything from presentation to outside broadcasts, often learning as you go along, with no formal training (Figure 2.2). There is also the gratification that you are performing a useful service for patients in hospital.

Facilities and the quality of output vary from station to station. One of the best ways to get a job in professional radio is to have a combination of local paper and hospital radio experience. If your hospital radio station does not have its own local news programme, why not offer to put one together?

Figure 2.2 Hospital radio is often a way in for future full-timers, but this presenter is just demonstrating that listeners can also become broadcasters! (Courtesy of the *Kent and Sussex Courier*).

College courses

There is now an increasing number of college courses devoted to teaching the skills of radio journalism. Again, there is a lot of competition for places but the standard of graduates is getting better. Courses fall into two main categories – postgraduate courses leading to a diploma or similar qualification, or three-year Communication and Media Studies courses leading to a degree. The latter combines studying radio with TV and other media, but both usually include short attachments with working BBC and IR newsrooms.

See the Appendix for addresses concerning radio courses.

Freelancing

Because of the competition, it is often difficult to find a staff job after college, local papers or hospital radio. One answer is to offer your services as a freelance radio journalist. You have to be adaptable, mobile and confident in your own abilities. It is not the option for you if you crave security, but it can be lucrative. You need to phone or write with a demo tape to news editors. Usually you will find that one job leads to others as you spread your own network of contacts. Remember – be persistent, have a good CV and demo tape (a good-quality cassette of you reading a news bulletin and examples of your work) and make sure that news editors know about the services you offer.

3

News-gathering

The newsroom structure

Newsrooms vary in size depending on the radio station. There is usually a similar structure of staff who do specific and necessary tasks (Figure 3.1).

Independent Radio	BBC Local Radio
Managing Director	Station Manager/Managing Editor
Programme Controller	Programme Organizer
Head of News/News Editor	News Editor
Deputy Head of News/News Editor	Bulletin Editor
Bulletin Editor	Senior Producer
Senior Journalists	Producers
Trainee Journalists	Reporters
Newsroom Assistant	News Production Assistant/ Newsroom Secretary

Figure 3.1 Newsroom structures.

Head of News or News Editor

This is the senior journalist in the newsroom reporting directly to the Programme Controller or Station Manager (or Managing Editor) who is editorially and managerially in charge.

Editorial jobs include:

- helping to decide the frequency and times of bulletins
- being responsible for the content
- deciding the proportion of local to national news
- making sure stories are legally safe
- deciding what stories should be covered and by whom
- dealing with complaints

Managerial jobs include:

- recruiting and motivating staff
- compiling rotas
- preparing a budget and working within it
- booking freelances
- arranging payments to agencies
- attending public relations functions

On some stations, the Head of News is involved in the day-to-day running of the newsdesk. In others, he or she deals more with administration.

Bulletin Editor

This is the duty journalist responsible for hourly supervision of the content and compilation of the bulletins. They will usually read the bulletins themselves and self-operate the desk. Other duties include:

- checking the latest from the emergency services – 'doing the calls'
- checking that copy and cues conform to style
- checking accuracy and legality of stories
- looking for follow-up angles
- making sure the story is fair and balanced
- re-writing and freshening stories
- allocating reporters to stories

Senior Journalist or Producer

Acts as Bulletin Editor when required, collecting and preparing news stories. The main difference between seniors and reporters is that seniors are more often concerned with making decisions, generating stories and thinking of angles than actually doing the reporting job.

Reporters

The Reporters are the 'firefighters' of the newsroom, following up stories, doing interviews and reporting from the scene. Their main job is to collect audio or actuality. The qualifications for the job include knowing what makes a good story, accuracy, persistence, speed and 'thinking radio' – the best way to cover a story in sound.

One-journalist newsrooms

Smaller stations operate with one or two journalists combining all these jobs. This is the way many American radio stations operate and may be the way forward for some British commercial radio stations. The main attributes needed here are a clear sense of priorities and doing as much as possible within the time available.

National news suppliers

A local radio station would be unconvincing indeed without local news. Equally, its news output must acknowledge there is a wide world beyond 'your patch'. The provision of national and international news for local radio is undertaken by several specialist organizations:

The BBC's General News Service (GNS). GNS supplies material to BBC local and regional stations by landline; it is not available to any other network.

Independent Radio News's (IRN). IRN was formed in 1973 at the start of Independent Radio in Britain. The service is available by SMS satellite, on subscription, to any IR station. Recently, local stations have been financing IRN by carrying special commercials on their behalf, called Newslink, rather than by making cash payments. Independent Television News (ITN) became involved with IRN in mid-1992

Network News. Network News was formed in mid-1991. It provides top-of-the-hour bulletins round the clock via the Intelsat satellite and is available on a similar basis to IRN. It is a live bulletin service only.

News agencies. The copy services of agencies such as the Press Association and Reuters are also used by some stations as additional sources, but they do not provide audio.

Radio news agencies, like their counterparts in newspapers, provide stories as they break. Because radio is a medium of sound, its agencies must provide not only copy but also appropriate actuality and voice pieces. The technical implications are that stations must be linked to their national agencies by two lines – one carrying the data to newsroom teleprinters or visual display units and the other providing the audio for use in bulletins.

The local intake systems

In practice, the result at the local end is that a dedicated printer produces a virtually continuous stream of copy. Meanwhile the BBC's GNS sends audio at 10 and 40 minutes past each hour, and IRN sends audio at 15, 30 and 45 minutes past the hour. Of course, a fast-breaking story may mean that audio arrives outside these times; most bulletin editors are familiar with the 'late feed' which arrives just a couple of minutes before the hourly bulletin.

The newsroom equipment consists, at minimum, of a teleprinter and a dedicated tape recorder (a 'logger'), as well as a cartridge recording stack. A simple electronic device switches on the tape recorder just before each piece of audio is sent and switches it off again afterwards. The audio, once captured on tape at the local end, can be dubbed onto cart for broadcast (see also 'Cartridges' in Chapter 6). It is possible to take the audio straight onto cart as it is fed from the agency, but the logging tape should still be running in case the first cart copy is unsuccessful.

BBC stations take automation one step further: a signal is fed just before each piece of audio which not only starts the logging tape but also starts a cart if one is inserted in the stack.

Teleprinters

Teleprinters do not just provide cues for audio. A typical hour will also produce some copy stories, at least one summary for headlines, financial news and perhaps a weather forecast. There will also be a variety of service messages: the teleprinter is used as a mailbox for the network and may carry all kinds of other information including news prospects and updated music charts.

It is part of the bulletin editor's job to assess all this information, either using it, passing it to someone else or throwing it away.

Live bulletins from agencies

IRN and Network News provide a two- or three-minute bulletin every hour, 24 hours a day, read from London, which can be taken live by local stations. Some IR stations use this and 'tag' their local news on the end. Others compile their own bulletins during the day, mixing local stories with the material sent from IRN. There is no equivalent service in the BBC.

Sources of local news

News arrives from many different sources:

- members of the public
- other radio station staff
- press releases
- pressure groups
- politicians and local councils
- freelance journalists and agencies
- the emergency services
- public utilities

When you get this information, you have to decide two questions: is it reliable, and is it newsworthy? If the answer to both is 'yes', you have a story.

'No' to the first question will mean further checking. For example, a member of the public reports a serious road accident. You must verify it with the police before using it.

'No' to the second question is the end of the matter. (But does this have any link with another story? Never be afraid to test decisions on your colleagues.)

Members of the public

All kinds of people can wander in with boring, rambling tales of rows with bosses or problems with noisy neighbours. Sometimes they bring a good story – but, if not, listen patiently and courteously. Even if they have wasted your time, express sympathy and give them the address of the local Citizens' Advice Bureau.

Other radio station staff

It has been said – truly – that everyone on a radio station should be a stringer for the newsroom. Independent station sales staff are out and about all day, so encourage them to call you with anything unusual. They are often the first to hear gossip about companies closing or expanding. Other staff, from the station manager or managing director downwards, can also come across stories by accident. Make sure they know you will be glad to listen.

Press releases

Press releases (Figure 3.2) need to be looked at carefully. They are distributed by people who want you to express a story in their terms. In reality, what they want to say may not be a story – for example, shops putting out 'press statements' about winter sales. Alternatively, it may be genuine news, but one-sided – for example, a release from a political party.

NEWS FROM THE BUCKSHEE GROUP

For Immediate Release 31st August 1992

Buckshee Technologies Ltd, a member of Buckshee International plc, is to transfer the production of hydraulic components from its factory in Newtown to its principal plant in Highworth. This decision follows a review of the company's manufacturing facilities in the light of changes in defence procurement and the continuing need to reduce, wherever possible, operating costs.

The Newtown plant will be closed and the 315 employees will be leaving the company. The company much regrets making this reduction in personnel and will provide job and financial counselling to assist those affected in finding alternative employment.

Note to Editors: Buckshee Technologies Ltd comprises a group of companies supplying the servicing control systems and components for the international aerospace and defence industries.

Enquiries to: Brian Johnson, Head of Media Relations, on 0908 269111.

Figure 3.2 Example of a press release from a company giving details of redundancies.

In most cases you will need to contact the source of the release to verify facts, get more information or set up an interview.

Telephoning people about their releases can be an education, particularly when public relations companies are involved. There are good, efficient PR companies who earn the fees they charge their clients and make covering a story easier. There are also incompetent firms who waste time and money all round. Be wary of any PR company sending out a press release to radio enclosing photographs (think about it!), referring to your 'readers', omitting phone numbers or forgetting the date.

When you make contact, perhaps the most idiotic response is: 'Why do you want to talk to anyone? It's all in the press release . . .', but others include: 'We could get someone to talk to you about this towards the end of next week', and 'You won't actually want to record this, will you?'

One more point: if the release comes from an 'amateur' source, you can be more forgiving about errors. Local people like pressure groups, religious organizations and charities do not know the rules like you do!

Pressure groups

Pressure groups simply want to put their side of the story as often as possible. Do not let them libel anyone and do your best to balance the story with the other side's views.

Politicians and local councils

Your MP will have the benefit of a formidable party media machine. There are no-holds-barred with MPs because they should be expert performers.

Local politicians are slightly different because the expertise of councillors varies widely. Some will be more effective than others. Do not overlook their usefulness when you want comments about a controversy. Also bear in mind that councillors are elected members and council officers are salaried staff who make recommendations to the members for decision. Both can be useful. Agenda and minutes from councils and health authorities are frequently tedious – but make sure you receive them and go through them, because a good story can lurk deep inside!

Freelance journalists and agencies

It would be impossible for most radio stations to cover the courts without copy from local freelance agencies. Equally, they can sometimes ferret out a story which has eluded you. However, do not feel hurt if a really good story finds its way to the national papers from a local agency – the big papers will pay hundreds of times the fee the agency can get from you. Beware of agencies who rewrite stories from the local papers. Also watch agencies who rewrite press releases – easy money for them but a pointless payment for you. Find out why you did not get the release; perhaps the sender was unaware of your existence. Overall you will benefit greatly from a good relationship with the local freelances.

The emergency services

The police, fire and ambulance services have a unique relationship with the media – both sides need the other. Regular check calls must be made, although sometimes you will be phoned by them (Figure 3.3).

Figure 3.3 A county police control room; one of the main sources of news on a regular basis. This is Northamptonshire – note the detailed map of the M1 (Courtesy of Bryan Hiley).

Make sure you have met the press officers in each service and that the relationship continues. If you do fall out (maybe a story was given to your rival station), make it your business to resume friendly relations as soon as possible.

A word of warning: the police do not always observe the laws of contempt and defamation as well as they might. Treat all information with care and subject it to the same legal tests as you would any other story.

Public utilities

The organizations which supply our electricity, gas, water and communications are all promising sources of news. As with the emergency services, be in regular touch with the relevant press officers. Make sure you have the names and numbers of local managers too, especially if the main press office is a long way away. Get to know them better by taking up invitations to see the locaal telephone exchange, sewage works or railway station. It takes some time, but it can be editorially rewarding – and there is usually some lunch laid on as well!

Planning and developing stories

The newsroom is likely to represent the biggest area of 'input' into a radio station. Press releases, letters, phone calls, tip-offs, telexes, faxes all arrive on the newsdesk. It is important to have suitable systems to assess the importance of these and file them away until needed.

The diary

The heart of a newsroom is its diary. All information about events supplied in advance is written in the diary under the appropriate date. It is up to everyone to put entries into the diary as soon as possible. Supporting papers such as the relevant council agenda, press release or letter are filed in the diary file – with numbers 1 to 31 corresponding to the days of the month. It should be the job of the reporter dealing with overnight stories (i.e. those for the next morning) to look through the diary and diary file and process previews of events happening the following day. On the day itself, it is the job of the duty news editor to assess what stories need covering within the resources available. It is important that the newsroom is highly organized in its copy flow and there is a tray or file allocated to receiving all this vital input from outside. This must be checked and processed regularly and not allowed to amass and overflow.

Resource management

With the information from the diary at hand, decisions need to be made about how stories can best be covered. In some newsrooms there are many staff and freelance reporters ready to be sent out on stories. Usually a newsroom conference is held to decide who does what, on what angle, and for when it is needed. In smaller newsrooms, it may simply be a case of deciding which story is worth following up by telephone by the one duty reporter.

The duty editor must always make allowances for the unexpected when planning coverage. Reporters may be allocated to cover the opening of a new hospital wing, a Royal visit, a council press conference or a controversial public meeting, but it is important to leave some leeway so that drastic, unforeseen events can be dealt with, such as an explosion or train crash. However, radio journalists cannot wait for stories to happen; they must act as well as react and pursue their own stories through their own contacts.

Developing stories

Reporters are allocated to specific stories. Each is briefed and given all the relevant background information from the diary file. It is the job of the duty editor to brief the reporter on the possible 'angles' and ways of treating the story. It is also important that each reporter is given a deadline so he or she knows exactly what is expected, by what time and in what form. There is no place or time in the newsroom for confusion.

Contacts book

A newsroom needs a system for finding the name and phone number of anyone in the news quickly. The best way to organize this is to create a contacts book – a simple A to Z index of people and organizations. It is a good rule that any phone number used by a journalist should be entered in the contacts book. This way a useful and comprehensive list of contacts is available speedily. It is important that the contacts are listed legibly, that everyone in the newsroom understands the system and what they have to do to find a number or put one in. For instance, all police phone numbers – including those of the force press officers – should be listed under 'police' and not under the individuals concerned.

Many newsrooms have succeeded or failed by the quality of their contacts book. In addition, journalists will inevitably develop their own books of personal contacts who have been particularly helpful to them or provide a useful source of stories.

'Rivals'

There is an attitude on some radio stations that rivals are not worth listening to. This could be a mistake. It is a journalist's job to know what other stations – or newspapers – are doing. But never 'lift' a story without checking it thoroughly first.

Story treatment

A news story can be dealt with in several ways for a bulletin:

Copylines

The quickest way to cover a story is simply as copy – that is, with no audio of any kind. Copy stories of a sentence or two are used for headlines; they are also a good way of making a bulletin sound busy, with several stories following each other quickly. If a story has been running with audio but you are reluctant to drop it entirely, reduce it to copy. However, a bulletin of nearly all copy sounds dull – it is no replacement for good audio.

Interviews

The classic way to cover a story for radio is to interview someone about it. Just who that is depends partly on you. You could, for example, decide to put a Labour accusation in the cue to a political story and have some audio from a Conservative denying it all – or the reverse.

Voice pieces or 'voicers'

Voicing a story is another way of doing it. It is less effective than an interview but sometimes the only way to improve on straight copy. In court cases, voicers are standard. Only rarely can you get audio about a court case – and virtually never while it is progressing because any comment could easily become contempt of court. The maximum duration of voice pieces varies slightly between the BBC and IR: BBC reporters aim at about 35 to 50 seconds, whereas IR likes 25 to 30 seconds at the most.

Cuts and clips

These are the same thing; a cut in IR and a clip in the BBC are both short pieces of audio. They could be part of an interview or an excerpt of a recording made on location – anything from a speech to a riot. Good clips have a start and a finish – they should not sound as though they have been taken from something longer. Again, acceptable duration is slightly longer at the BBC – up to 40 seconds or so. IR stations like no more than 30 seconds in most cases. A clip from an interview is much better if it has appropriate sound behind it, such as traffic behind a police officer talking about road accidents.

Wraps and packages

Once again, both words mean the same and are used in IR and the BBC respectively. The package consists of at least one clip surrounded by a reporter's voice. It can be short – a single clip of 10 seconds inserted in 20 seconds of reporter's voice to make 30 seconds. Alternatively a package can run three minutes or more for use in a news programme. They are an excellent way of putting both sides of an argument. For example:

> REPORTER: Angry parents lobbying County Hall this morning claimed that the increase in school meal prices will mean many children either starving or living on unhealthy

chips. Eileen Duncan . . . whose three children go to St John's Middle School in Moreton . . . says she can't possibly afford more than ten pounds a week for their lunches alone . . .

CLIP: Duncan act. 22″ Out: . . . absolute disgrace

REPORTER: But councillors on the education committee are defending the price rise. Conservative John Elliot says the meals are still to be subsidised at 72 pence a day . . .

CLIP: Elliot act. 25″ Out: . . . see reason

. . . and so on. The combination of scene-setting from the reporter and comment from people affected makes the story come alive.

Newsroom style book

You will have noticed that the names of types of audio and durations vary between the BBC and IR. In fact there are many more minor variations depending on local editors. Almost every station in either network develops its own 'house style'. For this reason a style book is helpful. It should set out the ground rules on durations, cue layout, cartridge labelling and many other small details that everyone in the news team follows instinctively after a while. The style book is an excellent point of reference if there is any uncertainty and makes life much easier for new staff members or occasional freelances working on shifts.

4

Writing technique

Writing for the ear and not the eye

Writing for the radio should reflect that you are *telling* the story to someone, not making ministerial-like pronouncements. You are not 'broadcasting' to the masses; simply explaining to an individual what is going on.

You should write in a clear, concise and non-stuffy way. Your words should not be the words of the sensational tabloid newspapers, but you should not be afraid of using informal language where it is appropriate.

Remember, you are writing for the ear and not the eye. You should write as you speak, in colloquial English, with short sentences and one thought per sentence.

People say: 'There's been a big fire at a shop in the town centre' not 'Firemen wearing breathing apparatus have been fighting a massive blaze at a retail store'.

Know what you want to say and say it conversationally, but do not use slang or be slapdash.

The first line

The first line must be short. It should hook the listener's attention while preparing him or her for a chain of events which are unfamiliar.

Do not make the mistake of trying to tell the whole story in the first line as newspaper style. It does not work in radio. Keep it simple. Keep it short. Keep it punchy. Then lead the listener through the story step-by-step and thought-by-thought, with each paragraph elaborating on the previous one. Try writing one long sentence followed by a short one, as this helps increase the pace.

Do not start with the most important words. People do not hear individual words on the radio but pick up groups of words or phrases.

Tenses

Radio's greatest strength is its immediacy. Therefore the use of the present tense – giving the impression that something is 'happening now' – is often appropriate, especially in the first line of stories.

Make sure you write in the present tense wherever possible. For example, 'Doctors have expressed surprise at the length of hospital waiting lists' becomes 'Doctors say they're surprised at the length of hospital waiting lists'.

If you are unable to use the present tense, you should make sure you write actively rather than passively. For example, 'A man has been charged by police' becomes 'Police have charged a man'.

Always think how you can write about what is happening now. For example, 'A woman's in hospital after . . .' or 'A family's waiting at the hospital bedside of . . .'.

Adjectives and colour

Many journalists try to amplify their stories by using too many adjectives. This has the effect of simply annoying the listener.

Facts should be treated with the utmost respect. For example, if we do not know that a fire 'ripped' through a building, then we should not say so (see also 'Bulletin essentials' in Chapter 5).

It is perfectly acceptable to add whatever 'colour' is available to a story. But if something did not happen in a certain way, you should not say it did just to liven up your story. It is far better to have a factually correct two-line story than a stunning couple of paragraphs which are exciting and racy but incorrect.

Writing devices

Radio writing does not always follow the textbook rules of English grammar. When you write for the ear, you are simply 'storing' words on paper so that you can tell someone later in the way you would speak. Therefore you need to use a number of writing devices to enable you to make sure that a script sounds as spontaneous as possible.

Contractions

You are *telling* the story; therefore what you write should use the normal contractions used in speech. For example:

It is	becomes	It'll
He is	becomes	He's
Do not	becomes	Don't
Should have	becomes	Should've
I am	becomes	I'm

At the start of sentences, it is also better to use a contraction when the third word is 'is'. For example: 'A man's going to make a record attempt . . .' or 'A hospital's appealing for more life-saving equipment . . .'.

Contractions make broadcasting sound much more natural and conversational.

Punctuation

Use punctuation devices to help you re-create in speech what you have written on paper. Full stops are, of course, essential. Do not use commas or dashes; use dots instead . . . like that! Do not try to read quotations on the radio, especially when they are long. This confuses the listener who may lose track of who is actually saying what. Is it the newsreader or the person he is reporting? Turn quotes into reported speech instead. There are certain times when it *is* acceptable to read quotes (see 'Quotations' in Chapter 5).

Jargon

Watch out for jargon when writing news stories. The sources of jargon are usually councils or the emergency services. For example, the police and ambulance service use terms like 'fractured femur' when we would say 'broken thigh'.

There are a whole host of other jargon words to watch out for from the police and fire brigade, such as:

Assistance (help)
Request (ask)
Terminate (end)
Decamped (ran off)
Released (cut free) (sent home)
Sustained injury (was hurt)
Absconded (escaped)

Councils are just as bad. Do not let council officers' jargon creep into your news stories. For example, a new building which, according to council papers, is 'detrimental to the visual amenity' is simply 'spoiling the view'.

Firefighters often use breathing apparatus. It keeps them alive. There is no need to say it all the time.

In road accidents (or what the police would call 'road traffic accidents'!) try to guard against attributing blame when describing what has happened. For example, 'A man's died after a car crashed into his motorbike on the M1' becomes 'A man's died after a car was in collision with his motorbike on the M1'.

The phrase 'in collision with' is a useful, though clumsy, way of making sure no blame is attributed, even if you are told the circumstances by official sources. Remember though that pedestrians are never 'in collision with' a car. To avoid sounding silly, use the phrase 'involved in an accident with'.

Journalese

A lot of shoddy radio writing is a legacy from newspapers and in particular 'headline English'. This sort of writing was developed by newspaper journalists because it consisted of short words which fitted into the confined space of a headline. These sort of words do not belong in a radio news bulletin:

too often we 'bid' instead of attempt
we 'slam' instead of criticize
we 'probe' instead of investigate
we 'axe' instead of cut
things are 'massive' instead of big
more things seem to 'plunge' than fall

Watch out for these words. You can find them most often in the freelance news copy which comes into radio newsrooms written by newspaper people anxious to 'sell' their story by the use of language like this. If it is there, rewrite it. It will sound much better.

Clichés

A phrase which has now become a cliché often began life as a useful piece of verbal shorthand. Unfortunately it has become overused to the point where it means nothing. Writing in clichés is a lazy, sloppy way of writing. Make sure you are never guilty of stringing a line of clichés together, even when you are under pressure (Figure 4.1).

Got under way	Blaze	Massive
Got off to a good start	Gutted	Mercy dash
A question mark hangs over	Rushed to hospital	Boss
Grind to a halt	Top secret	Chief
Turn the spotlight on	Grim	Watchdog
In the pipeline	Hit back	Decimate
Up in arms	Potentially lethal	Fulsome praise
At this moment in time	Slammed	Gunned down
The tip of the iceberg	Rapped	Too little, too late
The last straw	Bid	Only time will tell
The ball is in the other court	Probe	

Figure 4.1 A selection of well-worn clichés.

Americanisms

There are a lot of techniques we can learn from American radio, but the way Americans have changed the English language is not one of them!

Do watch for the more extreme Americanisms which appear regularly in films and TV drama. Words like 'hospitalized' are familiar on TV but they are not the words our listener would use.

Also try to avoid American pronunciations. One of the worst examples is the word 'schedule'. Often it is heard on the air as 'skedule'.

If we cannot get our own language correct, it says very little for our credibility!

Numbers and names

You should aim for a deliberately informal and conversational style. It should not therefore be necessary to use the prefixes 'Mr' and 'Mrs'. For example, John Major or Margaret Thatcher is perfectly acceptable. However, prefixes should be used in subsequent references, i.e., Mr Major or Mrs Thatcher.

Use Christian names rather than initials. If you cannot get a Christian name, it sounds better to leave out the name altogether, if possible, rather than using an initial which sounds very odd.

Numbers can be tricky to include in stories, especially when they are large. Only use figures when you must. The listener cannot always take in large sums.

Always write the numbers out so they are easy to read. Mixing words and figures makes it easy to see instantly what the amount is and how to say it:

400 000	becomes	400 thousand
4600	becomes	4 thousand 6 hundred
£50	becomes	50 pounds
£1.90	becomes	1 pound 90

Never use complex numbers. Always round up or down:

9.6	becomes	nearly 10 per cent
£4 898 785	becomes	almost 5 million pounds

To avoid figures, it often helps to use analogies such as 'the pile of rubbish is now as high as a double decker bus'.

Avoiding offence

We live in sensitive times. Many of the words and phrases which used to be employed freely are now no longer allowable in normal conversation, never mind news bulletins.

Never use offensive labels. Stick to the facts. If someone is black, then they are black, not coloured. Race is not the only thing which can cause problems. Sex is another. It is likely to upset some people if you assume that a certain group is all male (or all female). For example:

Firemen are at the scene . . .
Policemen are warning that . . .
The average nurse says she's not paid enough . . .

There are a number of alternatives:

'policemen' become 'police officers'
'firemen' become 'fire fighters'
'ambulancemen' become 'ambulance crews'
'housewives' become 'shoppers'

However, do not take things to an extreme, where the word is not likely to be used in everyday speech. For example, a reporter once referred to 'fishermen' as 'fisherfolk'!

Sexual matters can be difficult to describe. Obviously tabloid insults like 'queer' and 'poof' are out, but 'gay' has become an acceptable synonym for homosexual. If someone is homosexual, do not look for bland euphemisms. They will not thank you and neither will the listener.

Disabled people do not much care for words like 'crippled' either. Someone who has no legs is 'disabled' (better than 'handicapped') and has a 'disability'.

One more tricky area is politics. It is up to politicians to describe their allegiance. If they say they are 'Independent Conservatives' then you must not shorten that to Conservatives.

Be careful also of words like 'moderate', 'radical' and 'extremist'. Useful shorthand they may be, but it is not always for us to make these identifications.

Extremists, for example, can be a term of abuse. Leave the abuse to politicians – report it by all means, but do not join in, even by accident.

Check the meanings *and* impact of words you use. The government *is* technically 'a regime'. But the word is now often used as an insult and is better avoided. If in doubt, look it up. Every newsroom should have a good dictionary. Make it a working tool.

Putting stories in context

It is important that the listener hears the full story in its original context and is not misled by the way it is written. Remember you only get one chance on radio to put over a point. The listener cannot go back and hear what you just said, in the way he or she can reread a newspaper story.

You have a responsibility which is different from a newspaper writer. You select exactly what stories you want your listener to hear. In newspapers, there are many stories on a page, all with different styles and sizes of headlines to attract attention. On radio, the listener is presented with a single thread of material.

Attribution

Never start your story with an unattributed statement. It could sound like the opinion of the radio station. Especially in controversial matters, make sure the listener knows the source of the opinion being expressed at the beginning of the story.

For example, 'Most managers are mean. That's the finding of a new survey out today' becomes 'A new survey out today claims that most managers are mean'.

It also sounds much more natural and gives the listener a better idea of the authority behind the statement. For example, nobody would ever say in normal speech: 'The price of coffee's going up again, according to the grocer.' Instead you would say: 'The grocer says the price of coffee's going up again.' The same principle applies to radio writing, which is trying to achieve this kind of naturalness in speech.

Exaggeration

It becomes very easy sometimes to exaggerate somebody's case. For example, the most dangerous place is an in-line to a cut or a clip: 'Mr Wheeler is denying the claim', when all in fact he is saying is that there is no evidence to support it. The correct in-line in this case would be: 'Mr Wheeler says there's no proof of the claim.'

You should also aim for much more precision when using words commonly used in tabloid newspaper journalism:

Has the council 'angrily' rejected a claim against it, or just strongly?

Is a 'massive police hunt' really under way, or is it really a full-scale police search?

Is the union really 'split' or is it only a small group which is out of step?

Casualty figures

Always pick low estimates of casualty figures, especially in reporting major accidents or disasters. It does no harm to your authority if the death toll rises, but credibility is damaged when dead people come alive.

Organizations

It is not always necessary to give the full name of an organization, particularly those with long titles. For example, 'transport union' is acceptable for the 'Transport and General Workers' Union'.

Where initials are used, for example the CBI, the first reference in your story should always be prefaced by a brief description such as 'The employers' organization, the CBI' or 'The health service union, COHSE'.

Titles

It is more logical for a person's title to come before their name. For example, 'The council chairman Philip Wheeler', rather than 'Philip Wheeler, council chairman'.

5

The news bulletin

What to include

The news bulletin is the showcase of the radio journalist. It is the chance to give the listener a good idea of what is happening in just a few minutes.

The importance of relevance

The key consideration in whether or not to include an item in a bulletin is its relevance. Each story must earn its place in the bulletin by having an effect on the listener's life. That effect can be directly through, say, his community charge going up, or indirectly by something which triggers his emotions through sympathy or empathy.

When making editorial decisions, you should always ask yourself: What does this mean to my listener?

Be careful with world news on local radio. Some stations, especially BBC ones, have a policy of including as much international news as possible. But others, including many IR stations, prefer to concentrate on home news. A well-known test at a radio training centre used to give students a news story about Sri Lankan Tamils blockading a port. What was the relevance to the listener in Britain? Many thought it had little – until they found out it would affect supplies of tea!

Also watch stories which come from council chambers. Many of them are very dull tales of political infighting or things which people generally neither care about nor understand. Unless there is a story which really does affect someone outside the council (such as dustbins being collected, roads being built, schools being shut), think twice about covering it.

As a general rule, go with stories which affect people. Ditch those which do not.

Quality versus quantity

If a news item needs artificial support to help it stand up, it is not really worth telling.

It is an unfortunate fact that many local radio stations throw at their listener a barrage of dull and boring stories simply because they are trying to fill a 'quota' of local news. Quality should never suffer for the sake of quantity. The listener notices very soon.

'Localness'

You are working in local radio. Local stories must be just that. Try to emphasize the local angle in all your stories. For example: 'Police are warning women not to walk alone at night after a series of attacks. The call comes after three indecent assaults in Milton Keynes . . .' becomes 'Police in Milton Keynes are warning women not to walk alone at night after three indecent assaults . . .'.

Also try to get as many place names in your bulletins as possible by frequently including lots of short, two-line copy stories from around your area. It quickens the pace of a bulletin and makes your listener feel as though you are covering his town or village even though you do not always have reporters on the ground. If you find an excuse for giving a list of place names then do it, within reason.

The 'life' of a story

Stories need freshening as much as possible. If you are working on a story for the following morning's breakfast bulletins, try to provide an alternative cut or clip and cue with a different angle.

This helps provide variety in the bulletin. Generally, a story will last for no more than three consecutive broadcasts. After that, it should be dropped or rewritten completely. With constantly changing and fast-moving stories, it is easy to freshen each hour and the benefits of doing this – whatever the pressures in the newsroom – are enormous; the listener feels up to date from hour to hour.

Bulletin essentials

Accuracy

There is no excuse for sloppy, inaccurate reporting. You must check all the facts and make sure they are right. If the story comes from the police, make sure you have spoken to the right person – a duty inspector, station sergeant or press officer. If you are making factual statements, make sure you know your facts or check them.

The best advice is *Check, check and check again.* If accuracy falls down, so does the radio station's credibility – and with it your own journalistic reputation.

There is an old journalistic maxim which is still as relevant today as it was years ago: *When in doubt, find out – if still in doubt, leave it out.*

Taste

Be careful not to upset your listener unnecessarily with tasteless gory detail. Some things are gruesome and horrible enough. Remember that your listener may be eating, drinking or playing with the children while listening to the radio. Torsos being cut up or blood-and-guts stories just do not go down well at the breakfast table.

Never run a story just to excite your listener with sex or violence.

Naturally, when there are grounds for public concern, stories involving sex and violence have to be covered; for example, a child cruelty case which the social services department should have prevented. However, try to emphasize the reason for legitimate public concern.

When describing a rape, it is sufficient to say 'raped' rather than 'brutally' or 'violently' raped.

When you have to describe acts of violence, you should avoid excitable language. Remember understatement is often more effective and has more impact. For example: 'The man was blasted in the head with a sawn-off shotgun and left lying in a pool of blood' becomes 'A man came up behind him and shot him once in the head'.

Balance and fairness

It is the job of a radio newsroom to reflect all opinions and give people criticized on the air the opportunity to reply. A balance may not necessarily be achieved within one bulletin, but over a period of time. For example, if a protester criticizes the chairman of the education committee about a schools closure on the 8 am news bulletin on Monday morning, it would be appropriate to have the education committee chairman's reply to that on the 8 am news bulletin on Tuesday morning. This allows both sides of the argument to reach the same audience, albeit on consecutive days.

Comment

You should avoid commenting at all on any story. Your job is to be dispassionate and objective.

Cues

The cue into audio is the link between the reporter, the bulletin presenter and the listener. Ideally, the listener will understand exactly what the reporter is saying, through the medium of the presenter. However, this ideal may stand or fall by the quality of the cue.

Starting off

A good cue has the story 'up top', but not all in the first line. Cramming too much into a first line confuses the listener. For example: 'More than 200 beds are set to close at St John's

Hospital in the coming year because the district health authority has been forced to save over a million pounds to meet government spending targets.'

That is the essence of the story, but you probably had to read it twice to get the sense of it and anyone hearing the words read aloud would almost certainly lose track somewhere. Now consider: 'More than 200 beds are set to close at St John's Hospital because of government financial restrictions. The warning has come from the district health authority . . . which needs to save over a million pounds by the end of next year.'

By dividing the story into two shorter sentences it becomes much easier to understand first time round – and remember the listener has only one chance to hear it. By contrast, a newspaper story can be read again and again to get all the details.

Going into detail

Having started the story, you may need to expand on it slightly; but beware! If you make the cue too long, the listener may get bored with the story before the audio is played. A good cue provides the context for the audio which follows; it is not intended to tell the whole story unaided.

However, you may add something like: 'But the decision is angering some city councillors . . . who say the health authority is already struggling through lack of cash brought about by previous government rulings.'

This paragraph prepares us to hear an angry councillor. But try not to be led astray into exhaustive detail of previous spending cuts, a list of twelve other hospitals in the county already affected by economies, or what the BMA said about the government and the NHS last June. In a long newspaper article, they would all have their place, but you have perhaps one minute or less to tell the whole story – including the audio.

Into the audio

A good middle paragraph in a cue sets the stage for the audio which follows. We go into the actual audio with an 'in-line' like this: 'Labour's John Weston . . . who represents Witham ward

. . . says the government is trying to run down the health service at the expense of people in the area.'

The audio

The words of Mr Weston which follow should add something fresh. Avoid, at all costs, a 'double cue'. The above example would be a 'double cue' if his first words were: 'This government is trying to run down the NHS at the expense of people in the area'.

If those *were* his first words, we need an in-line like: 'Labour's John Weston . . . who represents Witham ward . . . says these new economies will hit everyone.'

A double cue should be avoided because it tells the listener exactly what he is about to hear, so taking all the dramatic impact out of the audio which follows. Radio news is all about impact.

The cue layout

Every radio station has its own style of cue sheet (Figure 5.1), but any cue should include the following:

- the date
- the reporter's name or initials
- a name for the story (the 'catchline' or 'slug')
- the cue itself
- the duration of the audio
- the out-cue of the audio
- the total running time of the story (read the cue to yourself to time it; or count three words to a second)
- any special notes to help the bulletin editor

Presentation

A good newsreader can make even dull stories sound reasonable, but a poor reader can kill a hot story by presenting it incompetently.

Harris 11.9.92 pm bulls
EMBARGOED UNTIL 1300

HOSPITAL/Weston

More than 200 beds are set to close at St John's Hospital . . . because of government spending restrictions.

The warning has come from the district health authority . . . which needs to save over a million pounds by the end of next year.

But the decision is angering some city councillors . . . who say the health authority is already struggling through lack of cash brought about by previous government rulings.

Labour's John Weston . . . who represents Witham ward . . . says the government is trying to run down the health service at the expense of local people . . .

CART: Hospital/Weston
DUR: 24″
OUT: . . . harder all the time. (50″)

Figure 5.1 A typical cue.

Sounding interested

A ground rule is that you must be interested in the material. That means *sound* interested. If you do not care – and let it show – the listener is very unlikely to bother either.

Understanding your material

You must understand every story in your bulletin. You depend heavily on the reporters who wrote the copy, but because you must understand news to present it, never hesitate to query something which is uncertain. If you have to ask about it, the chances are high that the listener, who cannot ask questions of anyone, will be left completely in the dark.

Checking first

Do not, unless there is no alternative, read copy on the air unseen. It is too easy to misread something and realize only as the words are leaving your mouth that you have placed completely the wrong emphasis on the story. Read all your copy, out loud in advance if you can. A few minutes spent on rehearsal are never wasted.

Technically speaking

A well-read bulletin can be spoilt by a silly technical mistake. For example, 'I'm sorry about that, we'll try to bring you that report in our next bulletin . . .'. or 'I'm sorry, that wasn't the Prime Minister . . . it was the Secretary of the Farmers' Union . . .'

These embarrassing and unprofessional slips can usually be avoided. If you 'drive' the bulletin yourself – *check* your carts. Are they all cued? Are they in the right order? Have you got them all? If someone else drives the bulletin, have they got all the audio? Do they understand the order in which the carts or tapes must be played? Do they know which story might be dropped if there is an overrun? It may be praiseworthy to 'get out' of a technical error with aplomb, but a thousand times better not to let it happen in the first place.

Breathing in . . .

There are a number of good books on voice production and if you have any doubts about your own abilities, read one of them. Be aware, though, that such books are frequently intended for actors, not broadcasters. There is not the same requirement to 'project' your voice on radio because the microphone will amplify it for you. So do not shout. But do sit up straight and breathe properly. This means a couple of deep inhalations before you start. If you try to speak with almost empty lungs, your voice will sound thin and strained and you will feel uncomfortable.

During the bulletin, remember to keep breathing! That sounds odd, perhaps, but the right place to breathe is at the end of a sentence – not halfway through it. Use audio as a chance to take a couple more deep breaths if you feel nervous. Deep breathing – within reason – has a curiously calming effect.

Keeping level

Strange rises and falls in your tone of voice will puzzle and maybe amuse the listener. Do not strain to speak much lower or higher than is comfortable for you. Also, steer midway between a monotone and 'singing' the bulletin.

Pronunciation

The BBC publishes an excellent pronunciation dictionary which is well worth having in the newsroom (you do not have to be a BBC station!). Unless you are sure, ask other people about unusual words – another good reason for checking your copy first. Listen, too, when other news bulletins are on. The chances are high that network radio and television will get it right because they have so many more resources on which to call if they need to check unusual words. Foreign names are the worst. As the last resort, if you are not sure, take a deep breath, say the word confidently as well as you can and carry on. If it is really unusual, the listener probably knows no better. But take the first chance you get to check it. Local place names on local radio stations *must* be pronounced correctly. Make sure your station has a phonetic list of the difficult or tricky names (Figure 5.2).

Be a listener

It is very difficult to know how you sound without listening to a recording. So make an 'aircheck' of your bulletins regularly. Record a bulletin every week or two and listen to it afterwards. It is not ego-tripping; it is sensible monitoring of your performance.

You and the microphone

The microphone is a sensitive piece of equipment which will amplify everything it can. That means your voice, your

NEWS PRONUNCIATIONS

Name	Country	Pronunciation
Parvez LATIF	UK	paarváyz lătéef
Zvid GAMSAKHURDIA	USSR (former)	zvee-ádd gamssă*ch*óordi-ă
SUKHUMI		soo*ch*óomi (-*ch* as in Sc. 'loch')
ZUGDIDI		zoog-dyéedi
Ruslan KHASBULATOV		rŏossláan *ch*assbŏolátŏf (-*ch* as in Sc. 'loch')
DUSCHANBE		dooshanbáy
Yevgeniy SHAPOSHNIKOV		yĕvgáyni sháapŏshnikŏf
Andrey KOZYREV		andráy kózzirĕf
CHADLI Bin Jadeed	Algeria	shádli bin jădéed (-j as in 'Jack')
Abasi MADANI		ăbáassi máddăni
Ali BELHAJJ		álee bell-hájj (-j as in 'Jack')
Mohammed BOUDIAF		mō-hámmĕd bood-yáaf
Hocine AIT-AHMED		hŏossáyn īt áa*ch*mĕd (-ī as in 'high')
Abdul Hamid MEHRI		ábdŏol hăméed mé-hri (-me as in 'met')
TEHIYA	Israel	te-hee-yáa
MOLEDET		moléddet
Yuval NE'EMAN		yoovál nay-ĕmáan
Rehavam ZE'EVI		rĕ*ch*ăvám zĕ-ayvée
Anand PANYARACHUN	Thailand	annúnn pún-yarrătchóon (-u as in 'but')
VO VAN KIET	Vietnam	vó vún kyétt (-u as in 'but')

Figure 5.2 The BBC daily pronunciation list (Courtesy of the BBC Pronunciation Research Unit).

breathing, the rustle of clothing, the squeak of a chair, the rustle of scripts and the clunk of a cart. So when a microphone is open, move and act with care.

Distance from the microphone is important. Too close and the smack of lips and pop of consonants will make the bulletin unpleasant to hear. Too far away and you will be curiously distant, with extra reverberation making listening difficult. Also if you are too far away, the increase in gain which will be necessary to compensate can make the microphone even more sensitive to other, unwanted noise.

Stressing

You can tell the listener which words are important in a story by stressing them. You are the interpreter of news for the listener and if you do not stress the appropriate words, the listener will not get the idea. You may also lose the listener's attention entirely.

For example, here is a news voicer:

> The Prime Minister arrived at 10 Downing Street early this morning to start his first day at work. He went in by the front door just after eight o'clock, refusing to respond to reporters, although he did give them a wave and a smile. One of his first tasks will be the formation of a new Cabinet. Last night there was mounting speculation that he is considering a major reshuffle and, during this morning, the arrivals of various party figures at Downing Street have been closely watched. Sources close to the Prime Minister say he is considering new people for the jobs of Chancellor and Foreign Secretary and of course he will have to find a new Transport Secretary. But so far, no names have been announced. This is John Smith at Downing Street.

What words would you stress? Underline those that you think are important with a pencil and then compare them to the version below.

Here is the same voicer, with good stress words emphasized. Do not worry if you did not get them all. Try reading the piece out loud, with your stresses, and then read it again with these:

> The *Prime Minister* arrived at 10 Downing Street *early* this morning to start his *first* day at work. He went in by the front door just after eight o'clock, *refusing* to respond to reporters, although he *did* give them a wave and a smile. One of his *first* tasks will be the formation of a new *Cabinet.* Last night there was *mounting* speculation that he is considering a *major* reshuffle and, during this morning, the *arrivals* of various party figures at Downing Street have been *closely* watched. Sources close to the Prime Minister say he is considering *new* people for the jobs of *Chancellor* and *Foreign* Secretary, and of course he will have to find a new Transport Secretary. But *so far, no* names have been announced. This is John Smith at Downing Street.

Notice that the stresses are very particular: *foreign* needs a stress (it is probably the first time that this particular job has been mentioned in the reshuffle), but *secretary* is a word used for a number of Cabinet posts and does not need such emphasis. Also, there is an implication that everyone already knows that a new Transport Secretary will be needed – so no stress on that phrase.

Making a stress is not simply a matter of speaking more loudly; try pausing slightly before a stress word – let it sink in for the listener.

Quotations

Quotations need a special kind of stress. For example, in the sentence: 'The Prime Minister accused the Opposition of "cowardice and hypocrisy" over the issue . . .' a pause on each side of the quotation helps to make it clearer that these were the Prime Minister's actual words.

Corrections

Sometimes, you simply get something wrong. It might be your fault because you mis-read the copy, or someone else's because their mistake was not seen in time. If you know as you say it that something is wrong, an immediate correction is best: '. . . that should be *forty two* thousand . . .'; or '. . . I'm sorry, that should be *Watford* football club . . .'.

Do not make a meal of any correction like this. Simply say it and carry on with the same tone of voice as before. If you sound worried or thrown off your stride, the listener is likely to take it more seriously too.

Going back to a story later in the bulletin because it was wrong the first time is more noticeable. This is an editorial decision, but if you have made a mistake and it could be serious, as in a court case, there is probably no alternative than to refer back to the story and broadcast the correction. *Do not* repeat the original mistake if you can help it – simply put the correction in context and keep it as simple as possible. For example, 'As you may have heard earlier in the bulletin, a man from Tolworth Cross was jailed for rape at the city's Crown Court today. We'd like to make it clear that his name was *John* Smith.'

6

Technicalities

The studio

A radio studio uses a number of sources of sound. These can include:

- microphones
- records
- compact discs
- open-reel tapes
- cartridges
- cassettes
- telephone lines

A studio mixing desk allows all these sources to be combined into a broadcast signal and sent to the transmitter. Which sources are present depends on the purpose of the studio.

The news studio

A news studio (Figure 6.1) will need one microphone as an absolute minimum. The traditional way of operating is to have a microphone turned on ('opened') and turned off ('closed') from elsewhere (a 'control room') where the operator can also bring in other sources as required.

This system has largely been replaced by a more complex news studio, intended to be operated by the news presenter throughout.

Figure 6.1 A 'talks' studio at BBC Ulster, complete with microphones, headphones and portable clock. Also, note the cue light on the table – it is more visible in front of the broadcaster than it would be on the wall (Courtesy of Tim Arnold).

This modern news studio contains at least a microphone, a cartridge playing stack (probably a three-slot type known as a triple-stack) and a small mixing desk to combine these sources on air.

A better equipped studio (Figure 6.2) will also have a second microphone, a record facility on one of the cartridge slots, an open-reel tape recorder, a telephone balancing unit and a means of bringing in the output from another studio or landline.

Such a studio can be used not only for live bulletins but also for recording interviews, recording carts (either from the microphone or off open-reel tape), conducting telephone interviews, recording packages and editing open-reel tape. A second microphone also makes a live voicer much easier, using a reporter in the studio with the bulletin presenter.

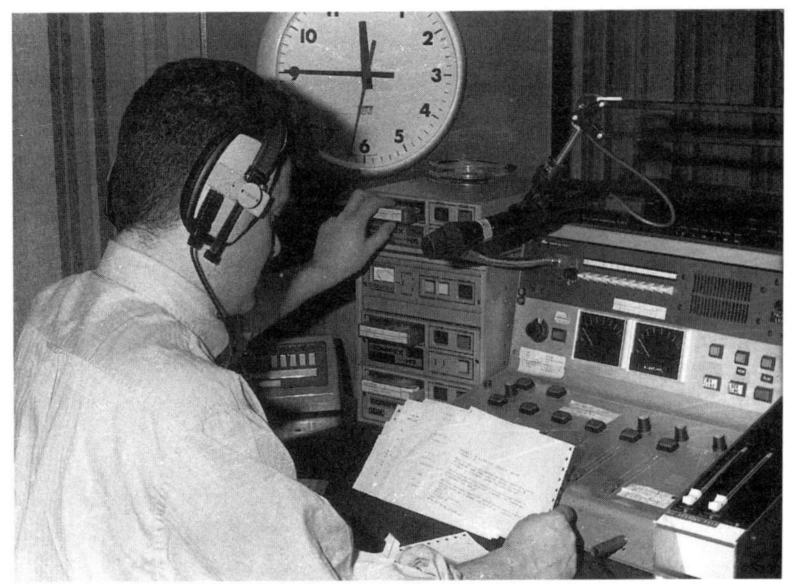

Figure 6.2 A purpose-built news presentation desk at Chiltern Radio.

Microphones

The choice of microphone for news will be fairly narrow, with a number of proven types tending to dominate the market. They include the Beyer M201 and AKG D202 which are all high-performance, directional types. An omnidirectional microphone is not a good choice for a news studio; it will tend to pick up stray noise from unwanted sources.

Cartridges

The broadcast cartridge (or 'cart') is a continuous loop of quarter-inch tape enclosed in a plastic case, rather like a square, oversize cassette. The running time can be anything from 10 seconds to 10 minutes. When a cart is recorded, an inaudible pulse is placed on the tape at the start point. The tape then runs until the same pulse is detected which causes it to stop, ready to play again at the touch of the 'play' button. Carts, therefore, are self-cueing devices.

Problems can arise if a cart is stopped manually ('potted'). When next started ('fired'), it will naturally begin from the same place, which could well be a silent section, or even midway through a voicer. A potted cart is therefore not cued, but there is no visual indication of this. To avoid the embarrassment of a dead cart on the air, all carts should be routinely re-cued at the end of a bulletin and so left ready for use again.

Some cart recording machines (Figure 6.3) can record more control pulses. A 'secondary' pulse is placed at the end of the recording; when detected, an appropriately equipped cart unit drops out of play mode and runs the tape at faster speed back to the cue point ('fast re-cue'). This is useful, but fast re-cueing sometimes causes increased motor noise and is not suitable for studios which also contain live microphones.

Usually, cart machines do not contain any kind of erase head. Carts are cleaned with a bulk erasing device, which generates a strong magnetic field. A cart used for recording without being

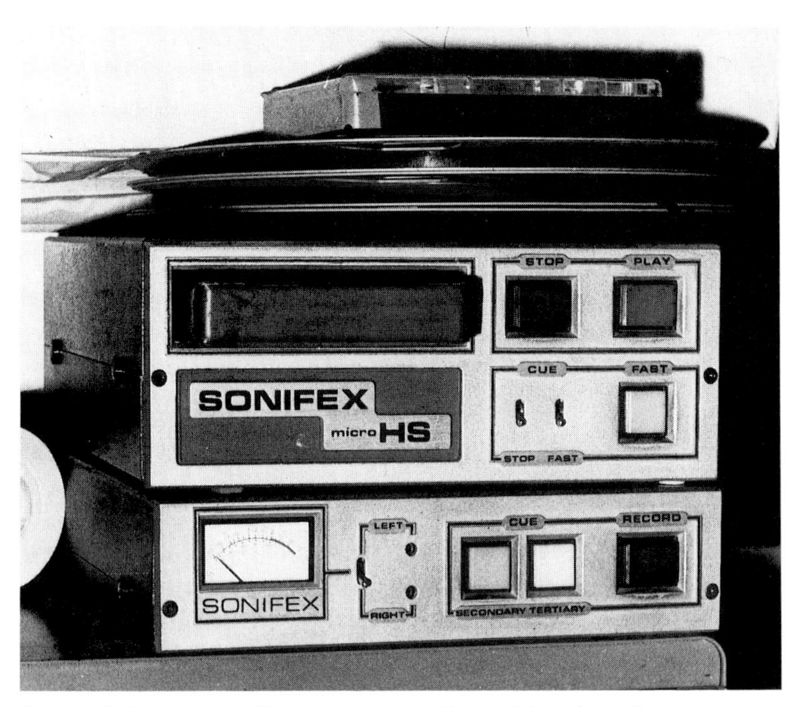

Figure 6.3 A modern cartridge stack, with recording module underneath.

cleaned or 'bulked' will retain the original recording underneath the new one and both will be heard. Such a cart is said to be 'dirty'. Some cart machines have a special erase mode, but this must be used before recording. The two functions cannot be used together.

Telephone balancing units

These are devices built into a studio desk allowing a telephone call to be brought up on a fader either to be recorded or broadcast live.

Tape recorders

All radio stations rely on different types of tape recorder (Figure 6.4) to conduct interviews and play out programme material.

How sound is recorded

The analogue recording of sound is achieved by using a device sensitive to variations in air pressure caused by sound waves – a microphone – to produce fluctuations in a very low electrical current. These fluctuations are passed to a recording head on the tape recorder, which generates a distinctive magnetic field. The particles of oxide on the passing tape are disturbed by this field and assume a new pattern in response. This pattern of oxide particles remains 'frozen' on the tape, until disturbed by another magnetic field.

If the tape is run past a playback head, the pattern of particles is 'read' by the head, which produces another current in turn. This current, duly amplified, is sent to a loudspeaker – broadly a microphone in reverse – so producing audible sound once again.

Although the current generated in a playback head is very similar to the original, various changes can occur during the process which are all technically known as 'distortion'. One major distortion of the reproduced signal is caused by background noise on the tape which cannot be entirely eliminated, although it has been reduced remarkably by ingenious circuits in modern analogue recorders.

Figure 6.4 The base model Revox tape recorder – a B77 with dust cover. Virtually the standard machine for newsrooms.

Digital recording

The newer process of digital recording largely overcomes the distortion problem by 'sampling' the frequencies of the signal, via microcircuitry. These values, recorded on the tape and played back through more microcircuitry, reproduce the original sound much more precisely than in the analogue process. Compact discs use this system.

Digital recording in radio stations is not yet very common, but its use is likely to spread in the next few years.

Speed

News tape recorders in radio stations use a standard speed of 7½ inches per second (i.p.s.). This speed is also used by cartridge machines, although, unlike cart stacks, open-reel recorders usually have at least two speeds. Slower speeds are not much used because quality suffers. Higher speeds are mainly used for music. Although speeds should be left set at 7½ i.p.s. on news machines, accidents can happen – so check, especially before playing a tape directly to air!

Recorders are generally full tape width stereo machines, adjusted for news purposes to use one track only. The other track is still recorded, but only with silence. This means you cannot turn the tape over and use it in the other direction.

Portable open-reel machines

Portable machines can be divided into open-reel and cassette types. The open-reel machines in use are usually Nagra or Uher models (Figure 6.5), running at 7½ i.p.s. These machines take

Figure 6.5 The Uher has been the standard open-reel portable machine for many years. It is rugged and well built, but is now replaced by cassette machines at some stations.

5-inch spools and record on half the tape width. They can be used in both directions if absolutely necessary, but this makes editing impossible unless you do not need the other track. Tape recorded in both directions also causes problems if reproduced on studio machines – the two tracks are heard simultaneously, one of them backwards.

Portable cassette machines

These machines are becoming more widespread, with some professional models now available no larger than the Sony Walkman. Popular models in use include Sony and Marantz (Figure 6.6). They allow 90 minutes of recording on a single

Figure 6.6 Marantz are one of the main suppliers of broadcast-quality cassette recorders. This is a lightweight and reliable machine.

cassette which can, of course, be turned over and used in both directions. With luck and ingenuity, it is possible to dub a clip straight from cassette to cart, but any changes mean you have to dub an intermediate copy onto quarter-inch tape, as cassettes themselves are difficult to edit. Cassette machines are much cheaper than open-reel portable models, costing perhaps only a quarter as much or even less.

Tape editing

Tape often has to be edited before transmission to remove unwanted parts of a recording (Figure 6.7). In an interview,

Figure 6.7 Editing a story at BBC Greater London Radio (Courtesy of Sarah Cavan).

people tend to cough, pause, make false starts and other mistakes; all these events are annoying for the listener and, if left untouched, would waste valuable time in a news bulletin.

Editing is never used to change the sense of an interview. It is not acceptable, for example, to splice together a question and answer which did not actually occur together in the original conversation.

You should interview in such a way that editing is reduced to a minimum. It takes a lot of time and tends to be more difficult to do just before the tape is wanted. The tension of an approaching deadline makes a lot of us less nimble-fingered.

Be careful with editing. Done properly, your expertise should not be noticed by the listener because a good edit goes unheard. That is one reason why tape recordings have been treated with caution for many years as potential legal evidence – they are too easy to change.

Taking care means listening to how your interviewee speaks, and making sure you preserve the natural rhythm of that speech by meticulously observing breath pauses. Two breaths spliced together sound ridiculous, but it is easily done. If, on the other hand, you remove all breath pauses in a sentence, the statements sound as if they have come from a robot. So, with editing, the golden rule is *listen twice – cut once*. In an ideal world, you would copy an interview and edit the copy, leaving the original untouched. In reality, there often is no time to make a copy, and perhaps you cannot get access to a pair of machines either.

The editing process

To edit, you will need – apart from your tape, a machine and headphones – the following tools:

- splicing tape
- a Chinagraph pencil
- a razor blade
- a splicing block

Splicing tape is specially made for the job. It is not too sticky and just narrower than the recording tape. Any other sticky tape cannot be used as a substitute. It may not stick properly, be too thick, or allow adhesive to leak onto the vulnerable heads of tape machines.

We will assume you need to edit 5 seconds of silence out of an interview. Place your machine in editing mode. This varies from model to model, but the aim is to hear the tape as you move it back and forth in front of the playback head.

Note that most professional machines have three heads. From left to right in the tape channel (the direction of tape travel) the heads are Erase, Record and Playback. You must edit on the Playback head, at the right of the channel.

Find the end of the audio you wish to keep and move the tape until you are just past it, by perhaps a quarter of a centimetre. Mark this spot using your Chinagraph pencil, making a short vertical line. Do not let your line stray off the sides of the tape – the pencil will mark the head itself just as easily and reduce the sound quality until it can be cleaned off again.

Now move the tape to the right, until you hear the next word which you wish to keep. Put a second mark just to the *right* of the word.

Remove the tape from the channel and put it along the splicing block. Using the 45-degree cut, cut the tape at each Chinagraph mark. Put the centre section (the short piece) on one side – do not lose it yet. Butt the free ends of the remaining tape together in the splicing block but do not overlap them (it is easily done!).

Place a piece of splicing tape about 3 centimetres long over the join, parallel with the tape and not overlapping it on either side. It is easiest to cut a length of splicing tape in advance and pick it up with the edge of your blade. Do not touch the splicing tape with your fingers more than necessary, as the oils in your skin will make it stick less well. Place over the join and press it down with your fingers. Then gently remove the tape from the block. The splicing tape should cover each side of the join equally. A good splice is as strong as the original tape. Finally, play back the spliced portion at normal speed. If all is well, you can now discard the short section you cut out. Figure 6.8 shows the splicing process.

If you want to add a pause, some wildtrack from the original interview is the proper solution, but if it must be silence, use blank tape and never coloured leader tape. That will not record and will ruin any future recordings made on the same tape.

Audio and actuality

The 'live' recording of a real event or person is usually called 'audio' in Independent Radio and 'actuality' in the BBC. It makes a bulletin sparkle and you should try to use it wherever it is justified.

Audio can be anything from a 17-second cut of the Prime Minister speaking in the Commons to a location interview with the fire chief in charge at a train crash.

Remember, though, that audio should add to a story. Think carefully about what it says and how it will fit into the overall story. Do not use audio just for the sake of it or simply to prove you were there.

Sound quality

Be careful about the sound quality of audio. If it is not good enough, do not use it. Try not to feel compelled to use an inferior

Aluminium splicing blocks have a channel for gripping the tape, and two cutting grooves of 45° and 90°

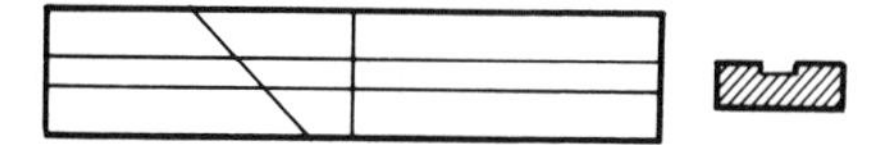

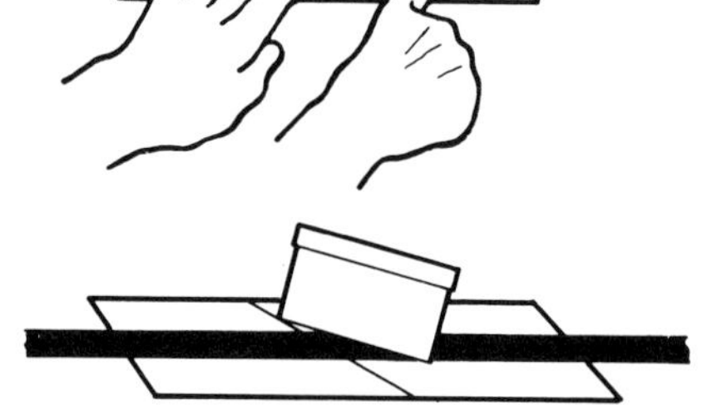

The tape is smoothed emulsion side down in the channel

Cutting marks are positioned over the 45° groove and a single-edged razor blade drawn across at angles of approximately 30°

Worn blades cause jagged cuts and damage cutting grooves

Wax pencil marks are removed before splicing

Professional splicing tape is fractionally narrower than magnetic tape

Tapes to be joined are butted together without overlap or gap

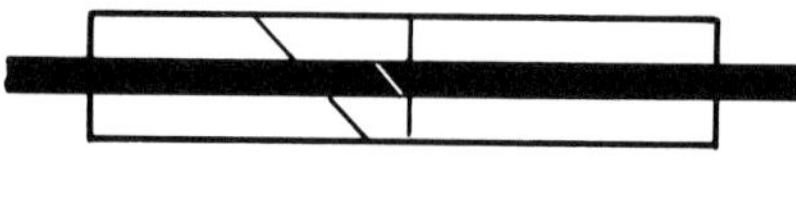

A short piece of splicing tape is placed on top (laying down one end first to avoid creases and air bubbles)

The splice is gently rubbed over to ensure good contact

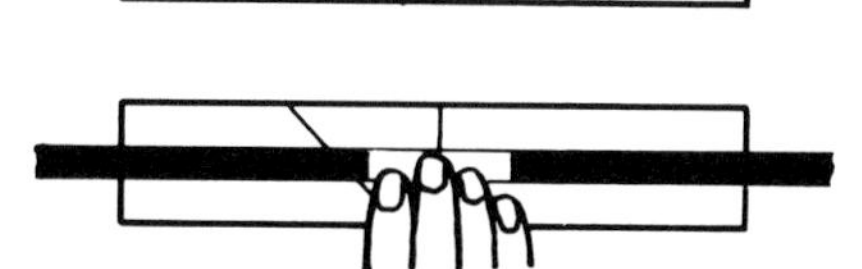

Tape is removed from the channel by pulling gently sideways

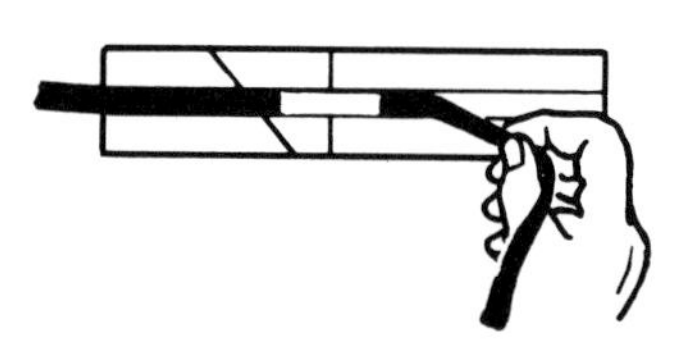

Figure 6.8 Splicing (From *Local Radio*, Focal Press, by courtesy of Barrie Redfern).

quality piece of audio just because of the effort which has gone into getting it. Remember that if you have trouble picking out what is being said when you are preparing the audio in the studio, by the time it reaches a transistor radio, it will make no sense at all.

Audio should be intelligible in itself and capable of being understood at the first hearing. If your listener has to spend two or three seconds trying to guess what is being said, you have failed. It is far better for the story to reach the listener as copy or a voicer rather than use inferior quality audio which cannot be understood.

Edits

Listen carefully to your selected piece of actuality and make sure every word is essential. Edit out really bad 'ers', 'ums' and stumbles, but be careful not to make the audio sound too unnatural and pay particular attention to making sure edits do not disrupt background noise.

Make sure all the edits are 'clean', with the correct breath pauses. If you need to edit the front of a piece of audio, splice in a section of blank tape, not leader tape, to make it sound clean. If you use leader, you will probably forget to remove it and it will stay there, waiting to spoil another recording.

'Carting'

Dubbing, or transferring, a piece of audio from open-reel tape to cartridge after editing is equally important. Make sure the carted audio also has a clean start without the first word being clipped with a 'wow' or 'zip' start. This is caused by insufficient care when the record start button is pressed on the cart machine. It is better to press this first, then start the open-reel audio a second later to give the cart machine time to activate.

Levels and equalization

The importance of good audio volume levels cannot be underestimated. It is silly to have spent time and effort preparing a story only to have it unheard by the listener because the volume is either too low or too high and distorted.

When audio is dubbed onto cartridge, it is vitally important that the volume level is set correctly. This is so that, when it comes to be played in a bulletin or programme, no further adjustment to the levels should be necessary.

Levels are measured in the studio by using a peak programme meter or PPM. Different stations have different rules about the level to which audio peaks, but generally you should aim at PPM 5¼ for the loudest sound. Telephone recordings contain a narrower band of frequencies, so the PPM for phone audio is slightly higher, to a maximum of PPM 6. The effect on volume is the same.

Equalization controls (EQ) on a studio mixing desk can be either a help or a hazard. They are glorified tone controls, similar but more sophisticated than the bass or treble knobs on a domestic hi-fi system. You can use them, for instance, to remove high frequencies such as tape hiss or the low frequencies of an air-conditioning system. They are also used to adjust tonal qualities of voices. However, you should be careful you know what you are doing; you may end up producing a muffled piece of audio which suffers from the same problem as low or high levels, i.e. the listener cannot hear it properly.

Telephone versus quality audio

There are two theories about this. It has been generally accepted that face-to-face audio quality is better than audio recorded over the phone. Remember it sounds far better to interview with background noise giving atmosphere, such as a busy office, a factory floor or a traffic-clogged street. This gives the impression of being 'busy'. Except where the background noise is excessive, it is hardly ever necessary to 'find a quiet corner' somewhere and record an interview. This will sound simply as if it had been recorded in a studio, which reduces the point of getting audio in the first place.

Phone audio has traditionally been thought of as a lazy and cheap way of doing interviews, avoiding the time and cost of travelling to a location. This is not necessarily the case and there has emerged a clear editorial justification for doing interviews like this.

Recent research shows that the listener does not mind phone cuts at all. In fact, he or she thinks the story is more 'immediate' if it is done on the phone. It sounds to them as if you have reacted fast to a story rather than done something which has required planning and a lot of time.

So phone audio not only makes use of radio's greatest asset – its immediacy – but also makes good economic sense for small stations with few staff and limited budgets.

Self-op bulletins

Traditionally, news on radio was read by one person with someone else performing the technical functions. This is still the case in some network stations, where a team can be involved in getting the bulletin to air. Some local stations still have someone other than the newsreader playing in the audio, opening the microphone and so on, but this person is often the presenter who is on duty anyway.

Increasingly the presenter at a local station presses a button or opens a fader marked 'News' at the appropriate moment and the bulletin presenter takes over entirely. And in some cases these days, the news studio actually takes control of the transmitters, switching out the main presentation studio, for the duration of the bulletin.

This section looks at the job of 'driving' the bulletin yourself.

Getting ready

If you are wise, you will be in the studio several minutes early. That is not because the bulletin might start early (it certainly should not!), but so that you can be ready to go. The best bulletins are not read, never mind driven, by someone who has just been pounding up a flight of stairs to the news studio with only seconds to spare.

Once in the studio, check the carts and cues again (this should have been done already in the newsroom). Do you have a set, or is a cue or cart missing? Another reason for arriving early is that any discrepancy found at this stage can be put right, if there is talkback to the newsroom. With luck, someone else can bring you the missing cart in time.

Insert the carts in the stack and, if the equipment allows it, fast re-cue them. (Be careful that you do not let this re-cueing process go on dangerously near the bulletin. You will feel foolish if your lead cart is still re-cueing when it is needed.) All carts should be cued anyway, but this is a good piece of extra insurance.

Check that the cues and carts are in the same order and that you are listening to the right output. If you are not getting the correct programme cue off air, you will not know when to begin and you may not be able to hear your own audio when you play it. In these days of multifrequency stations with split programming, getting the wrong programme cue is a real possibility. Once again, check in good time.

Here is the news . . .

Take a couple of deep breaths, then open your microphone while the news jingle – if there is one – is playing, not when it has faded out completely. The change in background sound will be less noticeable to listeners who have hi-fi equipment.

Start confidently, with one finger on the cart fire button for the first piece of audio.

As each piece of audio plays, if you have more than three inserts, 'update' the stack, by removing the spent carts and replacing them. Always have the next *two* carts ready. Should the first fail, the rattle of hastily inserted carts always sounds dreadful in a bulletin – so have another one ready to go.

If you are reading a bulletin which has a 'clock finish' (it ends at a precise time, to the second), keep the top two stories on one side where you can easily find them again, for reasons we will discuss shortly.

When things go wrong

If something fails in spite of all your precautions, *keep calm*. This is your bulletin and the listener will take a cue from you. If you are rattled or nervous, the listener will think something really serious has gone wrong. But do have some insurance. Have some extra copy stories with you that do not have to be used. Then, if you lose some audio, you have some extra material. It is not impossible for a complete cart stack to fail during a bulletin. With the cues and some extra copy, you should be able to keep going.

This is why we said keep the top two stories on one side. If you have to end precisely on time, or if a failure has left you ridiculously short, you can always refer back to them for the last 30 seconds of the bulletin (or even longer): '. . . and finally, the main stories again this hour . . .'. This may seem a gesture of desperation, but it actually sounds rather slick and urgent. The listener simply will not realize you are filling time if you sound confident. Some stations, incidentally, repeat the main story at the end of the bulletin as a matter of policy.

Only if all else fails should you end a bulletin early and then only if you are sure the succeeding programme is ready to take over. Nothing sounds worse than a silence after the bulletin. You are also unfairly giving the listener the impression that it is the next presenter who is in the wrong by not being ready.

If there is a failure, and it must be explained, do so in terms the listener will understand. *Never* say 'I'm sorry that cart wasn't cued . . .', but rather 'I'm sorry we can't bring you that report . . .'. The listener understandably thinks a cart is something pulled by a horse!

Remember that mistakes which are obvious enough to you may not be apparent to the listener. If you read a cue and the audio fails to fire, think before leaping in with an apology. A good audio cue will stand alone, if necessary. Do not apologise for something unless the failure is evident. If you can simply carry on, do so.

Computerized newsrooms

Benefits

The development of computerized newsrooms has moved quickly over the past few years. They give you the ability

- to access and rewrite stories easily
- to file stories after use

- to allow journalists in other centres to access your stories with ease
- to receive wire services and cues from IRN or GNS automatically and quickly
- to compile and time bulletins with ease
- to maintain updated lists of contacts to which everyone in the newsroom has access

The different systems

In Britain, there are two main systems in radio newsrooms. The first is Newstar, used by many commercial stations. This links in with IRN's system and allows national and international cues to be filed onto local terminals for retrieval by the duty bulletin editor. It can be rewritten as necessary or compiled into a bulletin with locally compiled material, and either printed out or read direct from the screen on air.

The second is the BBC's BASYS system which links many of its regional centres and local radio stations. This is similar to the Newstar system but there are differences, such as the styles of split-screen operation. Some people argue that BASYS offers too many features which are unnecessary for a local radio newsroom not operating as part of a large organization.

Other stations go for a cheaper and simpler option by setting up their own computer network. This can be done by linking together a group of personal computers and getting someone to write the appropriate software to bring news writing and newsroom administration together. The only problem with this is that there is no direct supply of national or international news – you are still tearing paper from a teleprinter.

Using the keyboard

Each computer system will have a number of basic features which will be found on the keyboard. Detailed instructions and the appropriate training should be given in each newsroom. However, among the features will be:

- a signing-on facility to enable you to link the local system into the national one

- screen formats for you to decide whether to display a full screen or split screen, making it easier to rewrite with the original on one half and your news version on the other
- mail systems to enable you to send material from one terminal to another or from one system to another
- 'help' keys to enable you to get a step-by-step guide to assistance if you are in trouble
- function keys for accessing story directories; reading, editing and creating a file; abstracting stories by specific criteria; combining stories; timing; searching for a word; archiving and filing; printing

7

Interviewing

Types of interview

The purpose of an interview is to get usable audio. This audio may be live or recorded. If it is recorded – which is more likely – the end result could be 15 seconds or several minutes. The cut itself could be used for a news bulletin, a package or a documentary. In spite of these varied uses, the principles of good interviewing are the same. But before you start, you should have a good idea of the type of interview you are about to do.

The informational interview

This is primarily to reveal facts or opinions. For example: 'How many ambulances are off the road because of a maintenance problem?'; 'Which way do you as MP intend to vote in tonight's crucial Commons vote?'; 'Why weren't the main roads in the county gritted before last night's frost?'

Note some of the words used above. The crucial words to use when asking questions are: *What*, *where*, *who*, *how*, *why*, and *when*. Questions starting with these words elicit answers other than just 'yes' or 'no', therefore making them much more useful on radio. They are known as 'open' questions. 'Closed' questions such as 'Do you think the county's roads were sufficiently gritted last night?' can lead to an interviewee simply saying 'yes' or 'no'. The interview intended to reveal information is most likely to achieve its object if the questions are short and direct but 'open'.

The interpretive interview

The interpretive interview is quite different. The subject of the interview needs to interpret some facts which are already known. The *fact* is that interest rates are rising again; the financial expert can be asked what *effect* this will have on mortgage rates. You should still, though, ask the question using the word 'what'. In this case, you are no longer dealing with an existing situation; the expert is being asked to look into the future and sketch the probabilities, usually based on knowledge of what has happened in similar circumstances before.

The emotional interview

The emotional interview is by far the most tricky type. Good reporting covers all shades and colours of human emotional experiences. There is the happiness of a sporting record breaker; the anxiety of a mother whose child is missing; the anger of a man who has been attacked and robbed. In an emotional interview, a certain amount of silence is more telling than any words, as the subject pauses to gather his or her thoughts, perhaps, in the midst of mental turmoil.

Journalists are sometime criticized for exploiting the emotions of others who may be in trouble or despair. In reality, no one can be compelled to talk if they do not wish to, and it has been said that people suffering in some way can find relief in recounting their feelings. After a big train or motorway crash, there is rarely a shortage of survivors who are anxious to tell their stories. It is often suggested by journalists that the act of describing a narrow escape seems to reduce the shock. However, that is not to condone the actions of a small minority of reporters – sometimes from newspapers – who undeniably overstep the bounds of decency in their determination to get a big 'tear-jerker'. The journalist has no licence to cause extra misery to people who are already suffering.

Interview preparation

If you are to ask sensible questions, you must know something of the subject. That is not to say that you need to be an expert yourself, but a few minutes of research is important beforehand.

However, you may well get pushed into an interview without any chance to prepare whatsoever. In that case, *use your interviewee* as a research resource. Let us say that you are about to interview a shop steward who is calling for a strike. You know little more than his name, his employer's name, and the union he represents. If you ask for an outright briefing before the interview, he may respect your honesty or he may feel contempt for your lack of knowledge, however unavoidable it may have been. So start with a wide-ranging question: 'Why do you think that a strike is now inevitable?' It is difficult to answer that question without giving a clue to the last offer from the employer! Now that you know the last offer was an extra 12%, you can go on to ask what would be acceptable and so on. The conversation has begun.

Location

You may carry out an interview almost anywhere. Most are recorded, but even live interviews can be conducted in many places outside the traditional studio. When you go out on location, make the most of the opportunities which may exist to include sound effects when these are relevant. Some well-meaning interviewees will offer you 'a quiet room'. They are rarely of any use unless they are a purpose-built studio. In particular, many rooms in offices and factories can be full of gloss-painted walls and hard metal objects. The resulting recording will sound as if it was made in a swimming bath, full of harsh echo.

The quiet room, even if it is reasonably well furnished and acoustically tolerable, still has one overwhelming defect – it is deadly boring. The point of going out on location is to paint a picture for the listener. Our colours are sound and our brush is a microphone, but the principles are the same. So question the airport manager with the sounds of jets taxiing on the tarmac in the background; interview the shop steward near the production line; talk to the teacher with children in the playground (if the school bell rings, carry on – it all adds spice!).

If all else fails, simply conduct the interview outside. The combination of birdsong, distant traffic, footsteps, the rustle of trees and similar sounds combine in what is sometimes known as 'exterior atmos(phere)'. Indeed, there are BBC sound effects records consisting of nothing else, which are intended to create a counterfeit exterior background for plays recorded in a studio. Exterior atmos is a curious phenomenon – we simply do not notice it in reality, but it jumps out of the radio!

You need to be aware of some dangers with sound effects. Do not let them be too loud or your interview will be drowned. Your interviewee may also be distracted and feel obliged to shout. Do realize that a continuous sound, like traffic, will make seamless editing almost impossible. The sound effect will change abruptly at every splice. And do not be tempted to add sounds which are not there! That is not objective reporting. It is acceptable, though, to record some extra sounds after an interview – say half a minute of the general background without any speech. Known as 'wildtrack', this clean sound can help if an edit is unavoidable, as it can be dubbed into the main recording to cover a splice.

'What did you have for breakfast . . . ?'

This question has gone into the lore of radio reporting. Newcomers – and some old hands – think it helps to ask the interviewee about the first meal of the day, to get some recording level and get the conversation going. It is all rather artificial and is better avoided – especially after one famous politician answered: 'An interviewer'! It is much more practical to ask the interviewee for his name and job title. You can take some level on that and your recording is immediately tagged with crucial information. Do not rely on sticky paper labels alone; they can fall off at vital moments.

A chat before the interview is fine – assuming you have the time. It is perfectly acceptable for the interviewee to ask what, in general, the piece will be about, if that is not already obvious. You can do a little more discreet research at the same time. But do not let an interviewee insist on a list of questions in advance. You cannot let yourself be tied in this way because, by agreeing to ask certain things, you are also agreeing not to raise other matters which may become more interesting as the interview progresses.

Watch their language

Of course, everyone should use words acceptable for broadcasting. But there is another kind of language – the language of the body. The interviewee may inadvertently reveal a lot about his mental state by his posture. Folded arms may be a sign of defensiveness; wringing hands, crossed legs and tapping fingers may reveal various states of tension. Tapping fingers, by the way, must be stopped with a courteous request. Otherwise the recording will probably be spoilt by a most peculiar thumping sound.

Question technique

You encourage an interviewee to talk by asking questions. That is your job. But do not be tempted into dominating the conversation – the listener wants to hear the voice of the interviewee rather than that of the interviewer. Below are a few general points.

Listening to answers

This is another good argument against prearranged questions. You *must* listen to what your subject has to say:

> SUBJECT: 'So a man of my height, just over six feet six, does have a real problem in finding clothes that fit.'
>
> REPORTER (not listening): 'So how tall are you then?'

Asking one thing at a time

Make an effort *not* to ramble:

> REPORTER: 'Would you say, then, that bus drivers have had enough, that is, that they are saying they aren't paid enough, so that they might take action – er, actually go on strike?'

Do not ask two or more questions in one:

REPORTER: 'Is it true that treating the roads cost the county more than thirty thousand pounds last winter and that you had to use salt as well as grit?'

Do not start quoting alternatives – then stop in mid-sentence:

REPORTER: 'Are you recommending to victims that they go to the police or the council or the Citizen's Advice Bureau or . . . ?'

Try not to interrupt, unless your subject is never going to stop until you intervene. Interruptions often sound untidy, and they are very difficult to edit sensibly into a short clip.

If you are in any doubt about suitable questions, remember the basics: *what*, *where*, *who*, *how*, *why*, and *when*. For example: 'What's happened?'; 'Where's the accident?'; 'Who's involved?'; 'How many people have been hurt?'; 'Why did the coach overturn?'; 'When will the road be clear?' There is no particular order of priority. It depends on the circumstances. However this kind of direct questioning will get you information quickly. Then you ask any necessary supplementary questions.

Eye contact

Encourage your subject with eye contact; it is friendly up to a point, but glance elsewhere now and then, otherwise it becomes aggressive. Use nods of the head to show that you are listening and understanding. Do *not* say 'yes . . .' or 'I see . . .' and other audible means of encouragement we use in conversation. Your words will be a real nuisance when the interview is played back. If you need to check your tape recorder – to confirm the level or make sure the tape is still rolling – then do so, but look back at your subject quickly. The interviewee will be disconcerted if you gaze elsewhere for long. He will think you are bored!

Leading questions

These questions encourage a certain answer and they are useful up to a point. Beware also that they are necessarily 'closed' type questions which could lead to a 'yes' or 'no' answer: 'So would you say that mothers must take extra care?'; 'You must be very angry about the decision?' Do not overdo these questions, as you are in danger of putting words into your subject's mouth.

Cliché questions

Think about your question technique. Each question you ask should serve a specific purpose. Do not fall into 'knee-jerk' interviewing habits:

REPORTER (to sobbing woman): 'How do you feel . . . ?'

After the interview

Do not go on longer than is reasonably necessary. Remember that you have got to listen to it all back afterwards. If you want a 30-second clip, 15 minutes is too much to put on tape. Five should be plenty and 10 more than ample. If you are after a clip and you hear what you want during the recording, wind up as soon as you can. There is no point in going on in the hope of something better.

Thanks

Remember to thank your subject. It is good public relations, as well as common courtesy, and you might need to talk to that person again in the future.

Special interviews

Live interviews

Live interviews are difficult. You may have just 1 minute allocated to a story. Get going quickly. Ask basic questions and keep them short. Interruptions may now be unavoidable, otherwise you may waste the whole interview on one answer.

Vox pops

Vox pops – literally *vox populi*, the voice of the people – are useful for lightweight subjects such as how people celebrate St Valentine's Day, or a breaking story of really universal interest like a cut in income tax. A good vox pop consists of short statements from members of the public, chosen at random in a street, edited neatly together in a stream of comments. Try to vary your subjects between young and old, male and female. The cue should make it absolutely clear what the question was. Out in the street, stick to that question and do not be drawn into a long interview with any one person. Names of interviewees are not necessary for once – and neither is it useful to name the reporter. Here is a sample cue, adapted from a real story about a Royal birth: 'Princess Louise's new baby girl is to be called Emily Jane Frances Victoria. The choice breaks with tradition as there's never been a member of the Royal Family called Emily before. We went out to see what people in the city think about Princess Emily . . .'.

If there is a clear majority of opinion on a controversial subject, your vox pop should echo that slant. If most people do not like the idea of a princess called Emily, then most of your clips should express the general opposition. Choose a humorous clip to end, if the subject allows.

Remember that not everyone likes being approached at random by a radio reporter. Keep smiling, stay courteous and do not pester people who do not want to know. If you are a nuisance, you will bring the name of your radio station into disrepute and you could be 'moved on' by police.

News conferences

These can be a free-for-all. Some are relatively well organized in a hall or conference room – even a church. Others are impromptu affairs on a doorstep, which start when a VIP emerges from a meeting. Do not be afraid to be at the front of the scrum. You and your microphone have just as much right as any other reporter. Television crews may not appreciate having your microphone in their shot – that is their tough luck. On the other hand, do not deliberately block their view with the back of your head.

If the VIP is going to say something once and disappear, you need the story just as much as anyone else, so be firm with any of your professional colleagues who try to elbow you out of the centre of the story because you are 'only local radio'. Sadly there are a few reporters who might try this, claiming they are more important. Do not be intimidated. In this game, everyone is equal.

At more organized news conferences, do not hesitate to request interview facilities. The organizers may be genuinely ignorant of radio's needs and suppose that questions shouted from the body of the hall will be adequate, as they can be for newspaper journalists. It is acceptable to 'share' recorded interviews on these occasions, if necessary. All radio reporters record at the same time and each one should get in a question or two. Do not worry if the result is a mixture of questioning voices, including reporters from 'the opposition'. Consult your editor, naturally, but as a general rule such interviews are dramatic and deserve a good piece of airtime.

Unattended studios

These are common in local radio and are frequently situated at civic centres and other public buildings in towns distant from the radio station. The unattended studio (sometimes called a 'remote') is linked to the main station by landline which gives good-quality speech transmission. The interviewer must frequently unlock a room and switch on the equipment inside. There is always a microphone, a telephone and usually some form of simple mixer. There should be clear instructions about what is to be switched on and what telephone number should be called so that the interviewee may report his arrival.

The interview itself is conducted with the landline carrying the interviewee's voice to the main radio station. Questions are usually asked via the telephone. If the questions are recorded simultaneously at the radio station end by the reporter through his own microphone, the result is a full 'quality' interview, even though the two parties may have been 20 or more miles apart.

8

The radio reporter

Reporting

The job of the reporter is to get the information, get it right and get it on the radio – fast. Radio reporters know where to go to get the information and who to talk to. They have an instinctive 'nose for news', ask lots of questions, are boundlessly enthusiastic and never give up until they have what they want.

Nowadays, it is usually the BBC and the bigger commercial stations who employ full-time reporters. In medium-sized commercial stations and the smaller community stations reporters are expected to combine their skills with newsreading and editing. Reporting is only one aspect of the job. But it is probably the most essential.

The briefing

All good reporters do their homework before going out on a story. It is useless for a reporter to be on a story without knowing background information. You should keep fully informed and check cuttings and previous stories, if available. To a certain extent, the newsdesk will be able to brief you when assigning you to a story. This may take the form of a complete file of previous stories, or may simply be a name, address or telephone number. Whatever, it is essential to think laterally and gather as much information as possible, within the timescale, before actually going out on the road.

Remember, driving time is also good thinking time (within reason). While you are driving to the story, think about what you want, what is expected of you and how you are going to tackle the subject. For a moment, forget all you have been told and ask yourself: What is this story really about?

Fixing ahead

There are two different sorts of basic reporting jobs. The first is a diary assignment – a function, event or interview notified to the newsdesk in advance, usually by a press release or phone call. For this, you need to arm yourself with the relevant background papers, read them and *think*.

You will usually be told (though sometimes it is up to you to decide) how much is required and in what form. For example, the launch of a new counselling service for AIDS sufferers may produce a 35-second bulletin wrap, a cut or clip alternative and a 4-minute package for a programme.

You will also be told when the various pieces are required. You could be sent out at 2 pm and told something is needed for the 4 pm news. Or, if it is not so important, the piece would simply be needed for the morning.

On this sort of job, most of the information about where and when to turn up is made available in advance. Sometimes a phone call is needed if you have particular interview or audio needs.

The other sort of job is the instant reaction callout. A bomb has exploded, a fire has started or a policeman has been shot. There is little time to think ahead or plan ahead. You simply get to the scene as quickly as possible and tell the story. If it is a big story requiring live coverage, your newsdesk will need not only to despatch you with the radio car but, in addition, arrange permission for access and parking.

Working to a deadline

It is important that you as the reporter know what your newsdesk needs and when it needs it. The deadline is all important. It is no use having a brilliant clip of audio and a stunning eyewitness account of an event if it misses the bulletin.

Know what is needed before you leave the office. Generally you will find that you work better having a deadline and being put under pressure.

In a major incident, it is important to stay in touch with the office as much as possible so that you can be told of changes in deadlines and requirements. News is about what is happening *now*. Your deadline could be five minutes before a bulletin or it could be while the bulletin is on the air as you do a live insert from a phone or radio car. Whatever it is, make sure you stick to the deadline and file something – anything – by that time.

On location

The story has broken, you have been briefed, told of your deadlines, researched any background, grabbed photocopies of previous stories, remembered to take a portable phone (and switch it on!), remembered to grab your portable tape recorder (with microphone, recharged batteries and tape!) and you are on

Figure 8.1 Arriving on location to cover a story. London taxis are popular with the BBC, partly because their tight turning circle makes them nimble in city traffic (Courtesy of Sarah Cavan).

your way through the traffic to the story, all the time thinking about what to do, how to do it and how to get the story on the air (Figure 8.1). You will be listening to your station's output, or that of your rivals, to glean as much up-to-date information being put out as possible.

What to do first

On arrival at the scene of the fire, explosion, shooting, or whatever, you have to assess the situation. Find out if the event is still happening or has finished. Make contact with the emergency services. Try to get an interview with the policeman or fire officer in charge straightaway. If it is a dramatic happening still continuing, ring base immediately. File a 'holding' voicer from the scene, describing what you can see. After you have done this, ask your newsdesk to contact the emergency services and find out who is in charge and enlist their cooperation. Then turn on your portable tape machine and start recording background noise – 'wildtrack' – for later use as a background to your piece. Record at least a couple of minutes. If there are explosions or shots keep the tape running.

Describe what is happening as you can see it and hear it. It does not matter if this is rubbish at first; just keep recording and talking without judging and you may be surprised at the results and what you will eventually be able to use.

Eyewitness accounts

Usually at these incidents there are bystanders watching what is going on. Try to find an eyewitness. Keep your tape running. Make sure you identify yourself, but get them talking in front of a microphone (Figure 8.2). Most people are only too happy to describe what they saw and what they did. You only need a few seconds of the most dramatic account. Ask questions. Do not forget, at the end, to get their name, and record it on your tape.

Dealing with officials

The emergency services have a job to do. Theirs is the most important job, not yours. They are in the business, in many cases, of saving lives. Let them get on with their own job. Try not

Figure 8.2 'Now tell me what you saw . . .' – getting the story for BBC Greater London Radio (Courtesy of Sarah Cavan).

to get in the way. However, watch out for firefighters who are resting, or police officers who are waiting and watching, and try to get instant reactions and descriptions from them. This will not always work and you will sometimes be told in no uncertain terms to go away.

In general, deal with the senior officers. If there is a press officer on the scene (which usually happens in major incidents), make sure he or she knows who you are and what you need. They will usually organize an on-the-spot briefing from a senior officer. Make sure you know when and where this is being held.

Always keep in touch with the newsdesk and tell them what is happening. Keep filing your eyewitness accounts and from-the-scene voicers.

Dealing with other reporters

It is up to you whether or not you associate with the scores of other television, radio and newspaper reporters who will turn up at a dramatic event. Usually it is best to work in a group and help each other out, although always being on the lookout for the exclusive eyewitness that the others have not spotted.

It helps to pool information, especially official information, to make sure everyone is broadcasting the same facts. Facts are sacred and not exclusive, but views, comments and interpretation can be up to you.

Filing back to base

Once you have arrived at the scene of a news story, it is important to get something on the air as soon as possible.

Getting on the air

Of course, the telephone is the best way of getting a story on the air quickly. The most flexible phone to use in these circumstances is a portable phone or carphone. If you have to use a payphone or callbox, reverse the charges and ask the operator to silence the pips, saying that you are working for a radio station. Beware that on some modern payphones it is impossible to silence the pips and incoming calls cannot be accepted. If you are covering a siege or other story which requires you to stay close to what is going on and do not have access to a mobile phone or payphone, knock on a few doors and see if there is a listener willing to let you use their phone.

You can enhance phone quality by using a frequency extender such as a Comrex, a device which boosts phone quality to almost broadcast quality. The old radio reporter's method of 'croc clipping' – that is, connecting wires from a portable tape recorder onto the inside mouthpiece of the phone, bypassing the poor-quality microphone – is now no longer possible as most modern handsets can be unscrewed.

By far the best way of getting on the air, however, is by using a radio car with a UHF transmitter, sending back material in studio quality.

On-the-spot voicers

If something dramatic is happening, try to ad-lib your report. This will convey the drama of the event. If you have time, script your piece or work from notes. Be sure your handwriting is clear. Many reporters have come to an embarrassing silence midway through a report because they cannot read their own scrawl! Try to sound dramatic, but do not go over the top and 'ham it up' too much. Do not shout, but sound forceful. End with a standard out cue (SOC), e.g. 'Stuart Miles, BBC News, Dover' or whatever your own station house style requires.

Live reports and questions-and-answers

Usually your piece will be pre-recorded. Sometimes it is better and more dramatic to do a live piece into a bulletin or programme. Make sure you can hear the off-air cue properly down the phone. Be sure you know when you will be needed and for how long. Try to get in a position where background noise can be heard. Again, remember the rules about working from a script if possible.

Questions-and-answers – Q and As (in Independent Radio) and two-ways (in the BBC) – happen where a presenter questions a reporter on the scene. If you are a reporter, make sure you are fully informed and up to date about what is happening. Try not to waffle just for the sake of it. Give the facts and do not speculate. Be responsible in what you say. Remember that in a siege, for example, a gunman could possibly have a radio tuned into your station and be listening to you describe the position of the police firearms team. If this is the case, you will not be able to tell any of your listeners the whole story. You are there to report what is happening, not influence it.

Q and As should be planned where possible, but if you are asked something about which you do not know the answer, say so.

'Car park' voicers

In certain circumstances it can help to enliven a script or story by recording it outside, maybe in your station's car park on a portable tape machine rather than in a studio. It is an effective production technique which creates an impression of being on the spot. However – do *not* claim in your standard out-cue that you *are* on location – one day you will be caught out.

Putting the material together

Once you have arrived back at base, having filed all your telephone or radio car pieces from site, you begin the daunting task of trying to assemble at least one short bulletin piece and a longer programme piece from what could be as much as 45 minutes' worth of pre-recorded material such as interviews and background effects.

Choosing the clip or cut

Remember the different ways of getting something on the air. You are probably first of all looking for an audio cut – a 20- or 25-second piece from an interview. Secondly, you are listening for an alternative audio cut and, thirdly, you need to wrap everything together. Do not forget the immense value of listening to everything you have recorded, in order to begin the selection process on the way back to the studio from the scene in the car or in a taxi. It saves valuable editing time if you can walk into the newsroom with a clear idea of what you are able to deliver and start work straightaway.

Choose the most dramatic quotes from the audio you have gathered. Use the audio to get across opinion, descriptions or interpretations. Concentrate on the facts in the cue. Do not edit so tightly that the audio sounds unnatural, and make the cuts long enough to register with the listener.

Choose a clip that has a proper start and ends decently – in other words, a self-contained statement. Do not choose a clip which starts 'But . . .' or 'Well . . .' (if you can help it). Try as far as possible to exclude your own voice. As you become more practised, you will develop an 'ear' for a clip, as soon as your subject says it, while recording.

Doing a wrap or package

You will first of all need to listen to all your audio and make notes about what bits you want to use. Choose and cart the clips, then the background audio or wildtrack, being careful to label the carts carefully. Write your script, then go into the studio and record the whole wrap in one go onto a reel-to-reel tape. You can tighten up the audio if necessary later on.

There is another method of putting a package together and this is the technique of recording everything onto tape in the order you need it, including your voice, and then editing it all together. This is more time consuming and gives you less flexibility for using individual audio cuts in other pieces later.

Be sure to know exactly what is wanted from you. By this, you should know whether it is for a bulletin or programme and how long it is supposed to be. You also need a deadline.

Try to make as much use of audio and background effects as you can. After all, sound is what radio is all about. Show sound off. The more the listener feels he or she is at the scene, the better.

Writing the cue

Do not include anything in your pre-recorded wrap or package which is likely to be out of date by the time it is broadcast, otherwise this will ensure you have the headache of a last-minute editing job. Make sure there is space for this information to be included in the cue.

It is particularly important, when material is coming in to a bulletin or programme editor at breakneck speed, to make sure all the technical information about duration and outcue is included and marked clearly both on the cue itself and the cart. Particularly make sure your piece is timed correctly.

9

Newsdesk management

Running the newsdesk

The newsdesk is the centre of the news operation (Figure 9.1). Information arrives in a varying flow, depending on the time of day. Peak times tend to be the early morning up to the 8 am bulletin; again in the hour up to 1 pm, and once more in the early evening from 4 pm. A big, breaking story can quickly generate numerous audio clips and a mountain of copy.

Getting organized

An untidy newsdesk can be a nightmare. The best stories can be mislaid at the last, crucial moment in a pile of disorganized copy.

So run a newsdesk as you would a military operation. Plastic office trays are good to contain copy as well as suitable racks for cartridges. Copy paper can be A4 or A5, but the smaller size is easier to handle. At least one carbonless copy is useful.

One tray is for current bulletin material. Some bulletin editors like to assemble the next bulletin in skeleton form at the front of such a tray, adding to it as the minutes go by.

In the last 15 minutes it is helpful to have some space to lay out the growing bulletin story by story, so that late items can be inserted in their appropriate places right up to the last possible moment.

Figure 9.1 The bulletin desk at BBC Greater London Radio. Note the General News Service logging tape machine and the cartridge stack to its left. The duty producer can use the loudspeaker to monitor station output or the material from GNS as it is fed (Courtesy of Sarah Cavan).

Another tray should contain stories from earlier in the same day which have been used and superseded. Do not let old copy stray too far – something in it could be needed to update a running story ('. . . just how many jobs are there at that company? We were quoting that figure this morning . . .'), and the contents of the 'used' tray will form the overnight 'clip-up' – the daily file of stories kept for reference.

If there is room, further trays can hold the cues for the national audio, if you use it, and also freelance copy.

Organizing cartridges

The cartridge rack can be organized in whatever way suits you best, but it can be useful to keep local and national carts in two separate sequences. IRN audio cuts are numbered; labelling the carts with the IRN number and keeping them in order saves valuable seconds.

Cart labelling is very important. Inadequate information can lead to the wrong cart being played on air. A label should show the catchline of the story – preferably just one word – as well as the name of the person speaking (or name of a reporter for a voicer), the duration and outcue (the last two or three words so that the newsreader can continue smoothly at the end of the audio). For example:

COMMONS/Major act.
23″ OUT: . . . they were in power

STRIKE/Harris voicer
28″ OUT: . . . early next week

There are various conventions for cart labelling. Different stations have their own habits, but generally 'fx' means a sound effect:

OUT: . . . (Laughter fx)

If a word or phase is said more than once, the repetition is shown as follows:

OUT: . . . their problem (×2)

The (×2) means that the newsreader will wait to hear that phrase twice before carrying on. Some stations use (rpt.) for the same purpose, but that does not cater for a word turning up three times – it can happen.

Another abbreviation is 'act.' for actuality – meaning a clip of an event, interview or speech, but not a reporter's voice.

Taking audio

The national agency used by your station will 'feed' audio at regular intervals, although a cut can turn up outside the schedule. This means that you should keep a constant ear on the agency output. Have some clean carts ready – newsdesks find lengths of 20, 35, 40 and maybe 50 inches most useful.

It is best to cart up the audio directly from the feed, but keep the logger tape running too. If you miss one, you can always run the tape back and dub it to the cart, but this takes more time.

Carts when played should start clean, with neither a long pause nor a 'clipped' front. A cart should be started ('fired') just *before* the audio to allow the stack to come up to speed. BBC stations have an advantage: GNS provides a cart firing pulse at the front of a news clip.

Deadlines

Be ruthless about deadlines. Five or so minutes before a bulletin, close it to new material and go into the studio. Do not worry about that updated audio which arrives two minutes to the hour. If you are single handed, you cannot be in the newsroom carting it and reading the bulletin in the studio simultaneously; and you might miss the start of the bulletin for the sake of one update, which would be a disaster. *The bulletin matters most*. In the end, the listener does not know what stories you have failed to carry, but he or she will notice if the bulletin sounds odd or is not there!

Finding the lead

Having a tidy newsdesk means that you can see what stories are available and you can move on to the next stage – putting the bulletin together.

The first decision is to choose the lead story. The lead will be the most important story – the one which, in your judgement, will be most likely to grab the listener's attention. Some leads choose themselves – the Prime Minister has just resigned, or hundreds of people have died in a plane crash, or the Russians have just landed a man on Mars.

But there are other days when there is no obvious top story. In this case, choose the best three or four, those that 'sound like leads', and cycle them in different bulletins. There is no rule that says the top two stories in the 10 am bulletin should not be reversed for the 11 am. However, the first words of the bulletin should be fresh. This may mean rewriting a story with a new cue, so go ahead and do it. What does sound bad is a 'lead' story which turned up in exactly the same form as the second story in the previous bulletin.

If you are looking for leads, pay close attention to the most recent TV news or bulletins on other radio stations, or even (especially in the early morning) what the newspapers are doing. There are limits to this; the tabloids may lead with a vicar-and-blonde-in-sex-romp story which is completely unsuitable for your radio station. If all the nationals agree on a lead (which is not that common), then they are probably right. Remember, though, that they wrote their stories several hours ago – look hard for an angle which will update the news for the breakfast audience.

One more point: if your bulletins are 'mixes' of national and local stories, do not be afraid to lead with local news when you can. A strike involving 200 people in a local factory may be more important in your area than a bigger industrial dispute elsewhere. Some radio stations lead with local stories as a matter of policy, but critics of this say rigid rules about local versus national can result in distorted bulletin priorities.

The rest of the bulletin

Stories in the rest of the bulletin are often easier to put in order once your lead is established. Remember that stories about the same general subject should be linked (' . . . and still on the subject of house prices . . .'). This works well if, in a mixed bulletin, you can follow a national piece with a local angle on the same story. Try to end with something light, curious or plain funny, but do not fret if there is nothing like that around. Try recapping the lead story again if your station does not forbid it: 'And the main story again . . .' has a pleasantly urgent ring, and also helps the listener who tuned in just after the start.

Follow that story . . .

Once you have carried a good story, do not let it lie down and die too quickly. Nothing sounds odder than a lead which unaccountably disappears from the next bulletin entirely. Move a story slowly down in successive bulletins before dropping it and keep your story fresh with rewrites. A story which had good audio can be run as copy only later in the day. Should a good new angle develop, your story might well move up again. A story further down the bulletin can be dropped for an hour or two and then brought back. Watch, too, your balance of local, national and international stories. A good mixed bulletin should contain all three, but in varying amounts depending on what is going on.

Flash that snap . . .

A really good story may not wait for the next scheduled bulletin. A 'snap' usually becomes a 'newsflash' on air. Keep snaps short, only run them when the news is really 'hot', and try not to break a story within a few minutes of the bulletin unless it is top priority. A decision on whether to snap should be taken by the editor, but it is the bulletin editor's responsibility to be on the alert for breaking stories, and refer them upwards if necessary.

The network

It is your local station's job to contribute to the network when a good story breaks locally. Where stations carry the national bulletin live, there is often a clash of interests.

A local story given to the network too quickly may turn up in the national bulletin and eclipse the local news which follows. This is a difficult situation, and one argument in favour of mixed bulletins. Some stations with a really good local story often mix their bulletins 'on demand', so that local listeners do not hear an excellent local story broken by a national newsreader.

Check calls

You may be working in a very small newsroom, but one vital job which cannot be neglected, if you are to keep the flow of news coming, is regular check calls to the emergency services. The police, fire and ambulance control rooms expect calls from the media, but since not everyone in these services is equally willing to pass on information (some police officers especially remember the days when they were instructed 'don't tell the Press anything'), it is wise to cross-check with all three services. In addition, the police may be called to a fire but they may not think it worth mentioning unless someone dies or it looks like arson. The fire service control, on the other hand, is more likely to give details of any callout, serious or not.

An up-to-date 'calls list' is a necessity. Increasingly, the emergency services have specialist press officers (in office hours at least), and a relatively new and useful development is the Media Line; a recorded update, intended for reporters only, and therefore on an ex-directory number.

Allocating reporters

If you are lucky, you may have one or more reporters available to follow up running stories. They are an expensive resource, so use them with care. Ask yourself whether it is more effective to send someone out on a single story which may take most of the morning or to give them several stories to chase from the newsroom, relying on telephone interviews. The right answer could be either option; it all depends on the merits of the individual stories.

Giving orders

The newsdesk producer (BBC) or bulletin editor (IR) has a relatively senior job. It follows that reporters will be taking orders and the producer should remember that people respond better to requests rather than demands. It is the producer's job to make the story clear to the reporter as far as possible. If you, as producer, have a particular angle in view, do not expect the reporter to read your mind. However, a good reporter, even if well briefed, will still be on the watch for other angles and may come back with something quite unexpected. It may not have been the way you saw the story initially, but do not be too quick to criticize. After all, the reporter on the spot should be better placed to judge a story. If that judgement really was in error, follow it up calmly later on, having made the best of what you were given at the time. Nothing is worse than a big row about what should have been (but now cannot) be done before you have to read a bulletin!

What comes first

Sometimes a quiet news day can explode into action with several apparently good stories breaking almost simultaneously. If that happens, stand back and consider what to do. Do not leap at the first thing to hand, because first may not be best. You must weigh up each potential story. Generally pursue the easier ones first. You may get two or three finished in a short time. Then concentrate on the more difficult and time-consuming possibilities. It is a mistake to let everything else drop for the sake of one attractive but elusive story. You could end up with nothing.

Coping in a crisis

Occasionally the pace goes on warming up until it is too hot for comfort. If a spectacular story breaks, you do have to let other things go, albeit reluctantly. Consider that if County Hall has just been burnt to the ground with 2000 council staff evacuated and the town centre sealed off, you will not have time in your bulletins for much else anyway.

Do not hesitate to call for help within the radio station itself. People who are not journalists are nevertheless excellent at staffing the phones when, say, a foot of snow brings your area to a standstill. Staff from the programme controller's office or the salesroom are often intrigued at a chance to 'have a go' at news, even if it is under strict supervision.

Allocate your real journalists with care, pursue the major angles first and always think in terms of the next bulletin – preferably the next two or three. Save one or two items just in case there is no time to get them later on. And do not overlook what is going out live – get a tape running on the output if the story has split over into the general programming.

Court reporting

Reporting legal proceedings is a skilled job and whole books have been written on the subject.

In practice, radio journalists seldom spend much time in

courts. Smaller stations cannot routinely afford to let their journalists sit in a press box for maybe hours while a case proceeds. Instead, court copy will be filed by news agencies. Their time is well spent because they can send a report of a single case to a number of different outlets – radio, TV and newspapers – and, of course, be paid for each one.

So radio journalists are most likely to deal with court copy written by someone else, filed by telephone, fax or telex. Such copy may be reduced to a couple of paragraphs or, if more interesting, written as a voicer.

Only in really major cases will most radio journalists go to court. Even in a big case, though, there is little point in allocating a radio reporter to court throughout the hearing. They cannot record the actual proceedings on tape for broadcast, and any interview with a witness or other person involved while a case is in progress would almost certainly constitute a serious contempt of court. Interviews with people involved in a case may be used after the trial is over, so long as what is said is not defamatory.

However the information is obtained, there are some basic rules of court reporting which must be followed scrupulously every time:

1. All court reports must identify accused persons beyond reasonable doubt, if they are to be named at all. Therefore, a name is rarely sufficient and the address should be given as well. The address may be abbreviated and a house or flat number is never used. It is usual, though not compulsory, to add an age and occupation.
2. It is illegal to identify certain defendants, such as children under 16 appearing in a juvenile court. A woman alleging rape is also entitled to anonymity. The former rule that a man accused of rape could not be named unless convicted has now been abolished. It is also possible for an order to be made witholding a defendant's name where publication could reasonably help to identify a child in the case, or where naming a witness could place him at risk. Such an order falls in the category of reporting restrictions and any journalist involved in court reporting must be aware if such restrictions apply. If they do, it is good practice to include in your copy that 'reporting restrictions were not lifted'.

3. The plea must be made clear. It is particularly important that any plea of not guilty is included in each report, but the actual words need not be used. A phrase such as 'Smith denies the charge . . .' is sufficient.
4. The charge or charges must be reported. In a complicated indictment, some abbreviation is customary in a radio report: 'Smith faces nine charges, including one of robbery, as well as insulting behaviour and breach of the peace . . .'.
5. Allegations reported must have actually been made in court and that fact must be made clear: 'The court was told that Smith had drunk seven pints of lager before the assault took place . . .'; 'The jury heard that Smith had visited the bank at least three times before the robbery . . .'. Such phrases as 'Prosecuting counsel told the jury . . .' are similarly acceptable.
6. Court reports must be balanced as far as possible. If you quote the prosecution case, you must say what the main line of defence is too (although not necessarily in the same report).
7. You must make it clear if your report comes midway through a case. Such reports customarily end with a phrase such as 'The case continues . . .' or 'The case is proceeding . . .'.
8. You must obey any special instruction of the court – for example that the name or address of a witness or defendant shall not be published. 'Published' includes broadcasting. It is the responsibility of a news agency to make sure that any instructions like this are included in their copy. Sometimes special points are included in a separate paragraph headed 'memo to newsdesk'. Read court copy *very* carefully, *all* the way through, and query anything doubtful immediately with the source. If a mistake is still broadcast, it is at least a partial defence to show that you took all reasonable steps to check the accuracy of the copy. However, there is no excuse for *ever* guessing any particulars in a court case. The old maxim applies – *if in doubt, leave it out*, even if it means dropping a doubtful story entirely for a bulletin until checks are made.
9. Although the proper place to check agency copy is with the agency, some court clerks are willing to help out by confirming, for example, when a case is likely to resume. Any information you get from a clerk, though, is your responsibility.

In summary, court reporting for radio usually means converting the copy of someone else who has been writing primarily for print. If you abridge a court report, make sure that you omit nothing which affects the balance by, say, leaving out the defence case. Above all else, ensure that your report is accurate, cannot prejudice a case which is proceeding or outstanding, and does not libel anyone.

The Law

Journalists do not have special rights under the law, except for a few occasions when a journalist has a legal right of access which is denied to the public – for example, at a juvenile court. In addition, some journalists have tested their traditionally proclaimed right to protect their sources, but not always with success. Generally, the journalist has the same rights and responsibilities as any citizen.

All journalists must have a working knowledge of certain areas of the law. There is room only for a brief summary here. McNae's *Essential Law for Journalists* by Tom Welsh and Walter Greenwood (Butterworths) gives more detail.

The two main areas likely to cause problems are *defamation* and *contempt of court*.

Defamation

The law says everyone has a right to a 'good name' throughout their lives, unless and until there is undeniable evidence to the contrary by, for example, being convicted of a crime.

Anything published which damages someone's reputation is potentially defamatory. Defamation is divided into *slander* (spoken) and *libel* (published). All broadcast defamation is defined as libel because broadcast speech is more wide-ranging than normal speech.

The other difference between slander and libel is that someone must normally suffer injury (for example, by losing their job) as a result of slander in order to win damages. There are a few exceptions to this general rule, but slander will rarely if ever trouble the broadcast journalist. So far as libel is concerned, mere proof of defamation is enough to win the case. The actual amount awarded, of course, can vary from trivial to extortionate.

Defences

1. The best defence to defamation is not to commit it in the first place. Remember that the comments of interviewees are not just their responsibility. You take on some of the blame by broadcasting them. Be on your guard for what people say.
2. Truth is a good defence – properly called 'justification'. But there are cases on record where someone has won damages even though the statements were accurate in themselves. Sometimes, this is because a listener could have drawn a defamatory conclusion from the way the facts were presented. The conclusions drawn by a reasonable person can certainly change if some facts are left out, for example.
3. It is also possible to defend an action for defamation by pleading *fair comment* (see below).
4. You can claim Privilege. Broadcasts of Parliamentary and council proceedings are protected by qualified privilege. This means that your report is safe so long as it is fair, accurate, without malice and broadcast contemporaneously – that is, as soon as possible. (You may sometimes hear that Parliamentary proceedings are protected by absolute privilege. This is true for the MPs in the chamber or the writers of Hansard, but not for you.)

   In the case of the courts, privilege is reckoned to be absolute, so long as a report is fair, accurate and contemporaneous. Absolute privilege is a complete defence to a libel action. The allegations reported, might, for example, be malicious and/or untrue, but if uttered in open court and accurately reported, that is an end of the matter.
5. There are two further main defences: (a) Accord and satisfaction and (b) Unintentional defamation. Accord and satisfaction would apply if an apology had already been broadcast and the plaintiff had agreed that it was acceptable redress. Unintentional defamation can result from an innocent confusion of names. It is one reason why the name of a defendant in a court report is rarely enough by itself – an indication of the address, age and perhaps occupation makes confusion with someone else less likely.

It is worth adding that libel actions cease with the death of the plaintiff, except in certain criminal libel cases (below). Also, a libel action cannot be brought more than three years after publication. Neither will it succeed if it can be shown that the plaintiff had agreed to the publication, but such proof could be difficult to obtain.

Criminal libel

Criminal libel is more serious still, and this charge can result from obscenity, sedition or blasphemy. A criminal libel action can also stem from a normal civil libel case, if a court decides that a defamation is so serious that it could lead to a breach of the peace. It is possible to criminally libel a dead person, if a court decides that the surviving relatives were likely to be provoked into breaching the peace as a result. The penalties for criminal libel include a prison sentence. If there is any suggestion of such a charge, get legal advice at once.

To summarise: the law of libel is complex, and there are a number of exceptions to the general rules. If in doubt, take legal advice or consult a specialist book on the subject – *before* the broadcast!

What is libellous?

Broadly speaking, libel is anything which damages someone's reputation. This includes accusations of dishonesty or incompetence, for example at a job or profession.

A group of people can be libelled without individual names being used. For example, 'Tory councillors in Blankshire are lining their pockets at Community Charge payers' expense. All the council contracts go to their friends.'

This is a plain accusation of a corrupt practice. Any Conservative councillor in Blankshire could claim damages.

Criticism and fair comment

Criticism is an essential part of the democratic process and is not necessarily libellous even if it descends to abuse, although you need to be on the alert. For example: 'Tory policies in Blankshire are hard-hearted and selfish. The poorest people in the community will once again be the losers while the rich will get richer. It's the same old miserable story of Damn You, Jack, I'm All Right.'

In the context of a reasonable debate, this is not a libellous statement. It is considered fair comment on a matter of public interest, and it is legally acceptable for people to express honest opinions and beliefs.

Despite there being no legal liability, you should give the Conservative group in Blankshire a chance to put their point of view in the interest of balance.

Be aware that some other words are potentially libellous and you should be careful how they are used and in what context. One of these is the word 'cruel'. Allegations of cruelty should be made only after very careful consideration. Also, make good use of the words 'claim' and 'allegation' in any story likely to prove controversial and critical of someone.

Reporting restrictions

An order not to publish or broadcast is known as a reporting restriction. The restriction may be statutory (as in the case of committal proceedings), or it may be made by a judge in a particular case. Statutory reporting restrictions, contained in Acts of Parliament, are intended to protect certain people. For example, a woman alleged to be the victim of a rape cannot be named and neither can children. (A child appearing on a joint charge with an adult before a Crown Court can be named in some circumstances. This is an unusual event, and the wise court reporter checks the exact position with the court before going ahead with publication.)

Judges and magistrates have the power to order special reporting restrictions in appropriate cases. For example, a judge may order that the name and address of a witness should be withheld if publication or broadcast would place him at risk.

Contempt of court

If you were foolish enough to ignore the reporting restrictions outlined previously, you could be found guilty of contempt of court.

The word contempt might suggest to you something like throwing tomatoes at a judge. While a judge would undoubtedly take a dim view of such conduct and probably impose a severe punishment, the meaning of contempt is rather wider than mere insulting behaviour.

Contempt of court includes any act which is likely to prejudice a forthcoming or current court hearing. To publish the evidence of someone involved in a case after they express it in court is lawful and proper (subject to reporting restrictions). But to publish the same evidence in advance would be contempt. If the witness actively helped with the advanced publication, or was paid, the court would take a very serious view and quite possibly jail the witness and those who published his words. Someone who also disobeys an order of the court can also be in contempt.

The penalty for contempt is not laid down by law. The theoretical maximum punishment is, therefore, an unlimited fine and a life sentence. In reality, it is not unknown for a contemptuous person to be jailed for an indefinite period. Lawyers say that the jail sentence ends when the guilty person has 'purged his contempt'. This means convincing a judge that he is truly sorry and will not repeat the offence. A formal apology in court is often required.

Criminal and civil cases are both covered by contempt law, but the criminal case is more carefully protected.

A step-by-step guide to contempt

Contempt is only possible at certain stages in a criminal case. To illustrate this, let us look at the foul and brutal murder of John Smith, found battered to death one wet Saturday night outside a pub. This is only intended as a guide. It is your responsibility to make sure you know as much detail as possible about what you can and cannot say.

Stage 1: Smith found by police. They appeal for witnesses. Nobody is in custody.

You can say what you like – as long as it is true, of course. A detective may give an interview describing the 'savage attack' and say he is launching a nationwide hunt for a 'dangerous killer who may strike again'.

Stage 2: Man arrested. It is the pub landlord. No charge yet.

You are immediately constrained. John Smith has now *not* been murdered. He has 'died'. It is *not* brutal. No adjectives are allowable at all. You should not identify the pub landlord, even if an incautious police officer tells you who has been arrested. You could write:

> Detectives in Blanktown have spent the night questioning a man in connection with the death of John Smith, whose body was found outside the Red Lion pub in West Street two days ago. Mr Smith, who was 42, lived in Cross Street, Blanktown. Police say they're likely to make a further statement later today.

Stage 3: Landlord due in court today, charged with murder.

The word 'murder' may now reappear because you are allowed to say what the charge is. However, other constraints stay. *Think carefully* before naming someone at this stage. What if the charge is withdrawn before the court appearance? The pub landlord could then sue for libel. You can say:

> A man is expected to appear before Blanktown magistrates today charged with the murder of 42-year-old John Smith whose body was found outside the Red Lion pub in West Street. Mr Smith lived in nearby Cross Street. His body was discovered by a police officer.

Stage 4: Landlord appears in Magistrates' Court for committal to Crown Court.

The rules change again. Generally you can now name him safely:

> A 53-year-old pub landlord from Blanktown has appeared before the town's magistrates charged with murder. George Jones . . . of the Red Lion in West Street . . . is accused of murdering John Smith of Cross Street in Blanktown. Mr Smith's body was found in West Street last Saturday night. Jones has been remanded in custody for seven days.

Stage 5: Case goes to Crown Court.

You may now report what happens each day in court and quote the judge, witnesses, counsel and the defendant himself. The words must have been said during the trial and must not be paraphrased in the report. They must be attributed and allegations clearly signposted by the use of such phrases as 'Prosecuting counsel alleged that . . .'; 'The judge warned the jury not to . . .'; 'The court was told that . . .'. The name of the court must be included, as well as an indication that the case is proceeding: 'The case continues'. Beware of interruptions from the public gallery. In general, these *must not* be reported in detail as they do not form part of the court proceedings and therefore will not be protected from any libel actions.

Stage 6: Jones found guilty of murder.

For the end of the case itself, the rules are the same as in stage 5:

> The judge told Jones that this was a savage and unprovoked attack . . . and a life sentence was inevitable. He also recommended that Jones should serve at least 20 years.

Stage 7: After the case.

You can almost go back to stage 1. You can broadcast a detective's opinion that 'Jones is a savage man who must stay behind bars for a long time'. You may interview relatives of the murderer or victim. They may say almost what they like, including criticism of the sentence. The usual rules of libel still apply. It must not, for example, be alleged that the judge, jury or counsel were dishonest, although a solicitor announcing an appeal can say what the grounds for appeal are. Also, Jones must not be accused of other crimes, unless he is facing further charges.

Civil cases

Civil law cases include any action between two or more parties which results from a conflict of some kind over rights, money or property. The border between civil and criminal bases is very carefully drawn, but it can be fairly narrow.

For example, to refuse to pay for food in a restaurant is not, in itself, a criminal act, in spite of anything the proprietor may say. If the refusal is caused by the low standards of food and if the complainant willingly identifies himself before leaving, it is up to the restaurant owner to sue for his money through the court. If, however, someone tries to leave surreptitiously without paying the bill, or orders food without the means to pay, that is a crime.

Common examples of civil cases include attempts to recover unpaid bills, the allocation of children's custody rights in divorce, and actions for defamation.

Civil cases are heard in the County Court or High Court, whereas criminal proceedings begin in a Magistrates' Court (in England and Wales) and proceed to Crown Court if the charge is serious enough. Criminal charges are generally brought by the Crown Prosecution Service following police action, but many civil cases involve arguments between two members of the public only.

A judge in a civil case may make an order in favour of the plaintiff or the defendant at the end of the hearing, and perhaps grant an injunction. This frequently prevents someone acting in a certain way and can be granted temporarily until a case can be fully aired in court. For example, a noisy family might be the subject of an injunction granted to neighbours forbidding them to have parties late at night. If the parties continue, those responsible are in contempt of court and may be punished.

Reporting a civil case involves much the same responsibility as in a criminal trial. Reports of what is said in court must be accurate. It is more difficult to be in contempt of a civil case by discussing it in advance, but take care. Before a civil case, you may outline the cause of the argument, but avoid a lot of detail and make sure that a summary of the disagreement is fairly presented. Steer clear of interviews with potential witnesses.

Inquests

An inquest is run by a coroner who is frequently medically qualified. His or her job is to discover the cause of death, where it may have been caused by accident or violence. Some serious cases – usually industrial accidents – may include a jury. A coroner sitting alone *records* a verdict. A coroner's jury *returns* a verdict. There are several verdicts which may be reached. They include death by accident, misadventure, justifiable homicide, unlawful killing and suicide. If the cause cannot be established, the result is an 'open' verdict.

Inquests cannot be prejudiced and there is no contempt in this sense. This is because an inquest is not trying to attach any blame to an individual. Beware, though, when reporting suspected suicides. If a man is found dead in his car with the engine running and a hosepipe from the exhaust fed through a window, you *must not* say it is suicide. That is for the coroner to decide. You can describe the circumstances in which the body was found and use phrases like: 'Police do not suspect foul play . . .'; 'Detectives say there are no suspicious circumstances . . .'; 'Police aren't looking for anyone else in connection with the incident . . .'. If it appears someone has shot himself, all you can say is that the body was found '. . . with a shotgun lying nearby'.

Official secrets

The issue of official secrets is very complex, but few radio journalists will come into conflict with it often. Journalists do not sign the Official Secrets Act but can be prosecuted for publishing information which might be useful to an enemy of the state.

The most usual contact between journalists and state secrets is the 'D-notice' (with D standing for Defence). This is a voluntary system which identifies sensitive subjects. It is set up by editors and government officials and overseen by a committee. The publication of a D-notice itself is restricted because they are confidential. Examples of the kind of subjects which could be covered are the locations of military sites, details of equipment on them, details of factories or products involved in defence, and the identities of certain Crown servants. Contravention of a D-notice is not an offence but it might well lead to further action.

10

Newsroom management

Setting up a small newsroom on a budget

Many smaller radio stations are now coming on the air. Although these stations have small budgets, it is still possible to set up an effective newsroom with just one or two journalists. However, the skills and organization needed are different from the way bigger newsrooms operate. The key thing to remember is that you cannot do everything, certainly not at once. Do not try. Learn to create priorities and deal with them in order.

Figure 10.1 gives a checklist of priorities for setting up a newsroom.

What to do first

When you are given the job of setting up a newsroom, you will usually find that the radio station is far from ready. Building work will be going on all around you and you will be lucky if you even have access to a telephone.

You need to create your own space – one room preferably – with a telephone, desk, chair, typewriter (or word processor), a supply of headed notepaper, an A-Z book for contacts, a large diary and filing cabinet. Of course, this needs to be complemented eventually by a tape recorder and other necessary technical equipment to get on the air (see below). You can then start the main job of talking to people and getting a flow of news

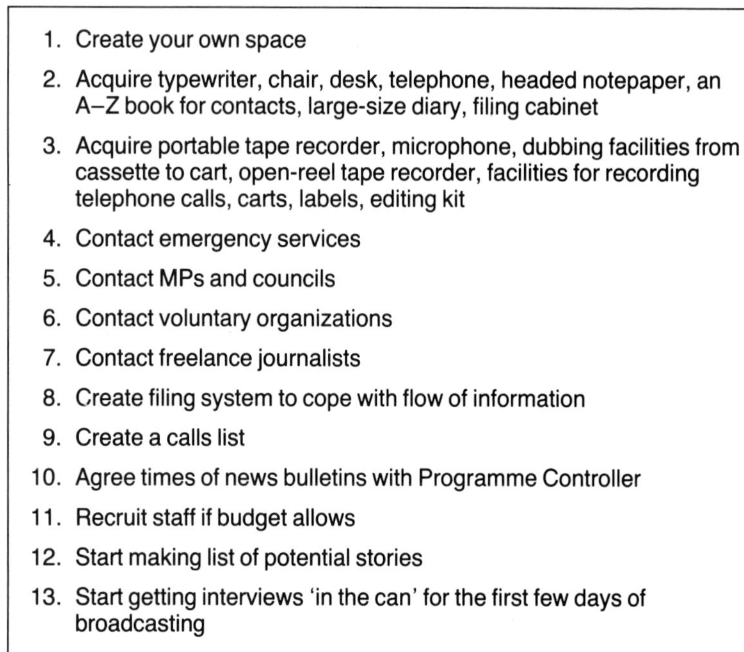

1. Create your own space
2. Acquire typewriter, chair, desk, telephone, headed notepaper, an A–Z book for contacts, large-size diary, filing cabinet
3. Acquire portable tape recorder, microphone, dubbing facilities from cassette to cart, open-reel tape recorder, facilities for recording telephone calls, carts, labels, editing kit
4. Contact emergency services
5. Contact MPs and councils
6. Contact voluntary organizations
7. Contact freelance journalists
8. Create filing system to cope with flow of information
9. Create a calls list
10. Agree times of news bulletins with Programme Controller
11. Recruit staff if budget allows
12. Start making list of potential stories
13. Start getting interviews 'in the can' for the first few days of broadcasting
14. Look for an exclusive or two for the first day's broadcasting
15. Start dummy-running news bulletins using your calls list and writing from press releases and conducting follow-up interviews

Figure 10.1 Checklist for setting up a newsroom.

coming in to the radio station. Ideally you need at least three weeks for this, although it has been done in less time.

Making contacts

Your main task, after setting up the newsroom, must be to let people know who you are, when you will be broadcasting and how to get in touch with you.

In the first instance, you should target the emergency services (police, fire, ambulance), the councils and local MPs. Your next priority after that is to contact as many voluntary organizations as possible. You will also need to acquaint yourself with local freelance journalists and news agencies.

It is usually worth phoning the emergency services' press officers, if they have them. You will probably need to visit them. You should have a list of your telephone numbers and take some radio station publicity material with you. Try to make friends with them. Bear in mind they will have other priorities as far as the press and broadcasters are concerned and you will be an unknown quantity. Tell them about the station, its target audience, on air date, its journalist(s) and what help you need from them. It is important to agree a set of times you can do check calls with them.

You need also to visit the press offices of the local district and county councils. Arrange for your address to be added to their mailing lists so you can receive council papers, agenda, minutes and press releases. Ask if you can write a letter to all their members. Do this, photocopy it and ask if the council could include it in their next mailshot. It needs to tell people you exist and how to get in contact with you.

Also write to the MPs with the same information. Make contact with the local voluntary organizations. Usually there is an 'umbrella' organization to which all voluntary groups in an area belong. Ask them if you can write a circular letter to their member groups which they can distribute in their next mailshot.

All the time you need to be selling your station, its potential audience and yourself. You need to be promoting the ways in which radio in general, and your station in particular, can help them. Very soon, you will have an impressive flow of news into your new newsroom.

Technical requirements

The minimum you need is a portable tape recorder and microphone, facilities for dubbing from cassette onto cartridge and edit via a reel-to-reel tape recorder, facilities for recording telephone interviews, a studio where you can record face-to-face interviews, and a good supply of carts, labels and editing kit.

Creating a filing system

With the amount of press releases and council papers flowing into your new newsroom, you need to set up a proper filing system to cope with it all. You need the following files:

1 *Diary file.* Two sets of files labelled 1 to 31, corresponding to the days of the month. Use one set for this month, the other for next month. Set aside a special file for beyond that. As events come into the newsroom, enter them under the appropriate date in the desk diary and file the relevant paperwork under the date in your file.
2. *Archive files.* Once you are on the air, you need to file all your bulletin and voicer scripts for reference purposes. There are a number of ways of doing this. One of the easiest is to have a ring-binder file for each month and file the copy there after each day's broadcasting.
3 *Contacts file.* Some newsrooms prefer to list names and phone numbers of contacts in a book with an A–Z index. Choose whichever system suits you the best.
4 *Background file.* File background information, newspaper cuttings, press releases and so on under the appropriate heading. Have a file for each council and emergency service, as well as files on such subjects as schools, buses, trains and specific running stories.
5 *Letters file.* Keep a copy of each letter you send as well as any you receive. Subject headings help.

There is also one more file – arguably the most important of all. It is the 'circular file', i.e. the dustbin. In the early days of a newsroom it is important to keep as much as possible because you never know what may be useful, but you will start to receive unsolicited commercial junk releases which have no relevance to your audience at all. Throw them away. But be careful to read *everything* you receive. You never know where a good story may be lurking!

Creating a calls list

Your list of calls to the emergency services either needs writing down on paper or displaying on a large easy-to-read black or white board. It needs to have the phone numbers of all the emergency services and, where possible, the officer who has the responsibility of talking to the press and radio. Direct lines need to be included where possible.

Police

Devon & Cornwall HQ	**52101**
Public relations, Information room, CID, Burglary Squad	
Dorset HQ	**0202 22099**
Dorset Press line	**0426 932435**
Avon & Somerset Yeovil	**0935 75291**
HQ	0272 27777
Roads	0225 9434
Barnstaple Control	**0271 7391**
Paignton Control	**0803 19201**

Local police stations

Ashburton	0364 95221
Bideford	0237 86896
Bridport	0308 2246
Budleigh Salterton	954 1431
Chard	04606 11300
Crediton	03632 92230
Dartmouth	0803 132288
Dawlish	0626 16331
Exeter Heavitree Rd.	910199
Exmouth	0395 14651
Honiton	0404 12171
Ivybridge	0752 8929
Newton Abbot	0626 594444
Okehampton	0837 2201
Seaton	0297 2763
Sidmouth	0395 5126
Teignmouth	0626 7433
Tiverton	0884 52323
Torquay	0803 14491

Fire

Devon	**87119**
Dorset Press line	**0426 122030**
Dorset Enquiries	0305 55599 **(urgent calls only)**
Somerset Press line	**0823 19901**

Ambulance

Devon Exeter	**43313**
Devon Torquay	**0803 61091**
Dorset	**0202 96689**
Somerset	**0823 8892**

Coastguard

Brixham South Devon	**0803 182704**
Portland E.Devon/Dorset	**0305 16149**

Figure 10.2 A typical calls list.

When setting up the list and going to see the emergency services, try to agree the following times to include them in a 'round of calls' (this is for a station broadcasting news bulletins from 6 am to 3 pm daily): 5 am, 9 am, 12 noon, 2 pm, 5 pm.

The important thing is to make sure the frequency of the calls is sufficient to satisfy your editorial needs without making yourself too much of a nuisance.

Many police forces and fire brigades now have pre-recorded 'press information' phone lines which can be helpful in getting basic information. These numbers should also be included on your calls list (Figure 10.2).

Recruiting staff

Your station may only have the budget to employ you in the newsroom or you may be lucky enough to have the money to recruit other people. If the latter is the case, it is likely that you will have come to the area experienced in broadcasting but without local knowledge. It is therefore important to recruit someone with that essential local knowledge.

The best place to try is the local newspaper. You will probably have contact with these journalists in any case as they will be writing stories about the new radio station for their own papers. Always be on the lookout for the newspaper journalist who has an interest in radio and is looking for a break.

If the budget allows, try advertising in the trade press. Care is needed in wording the ad. You need to be specific about duties, responsibilities, opportunities and salary.

Try to compile a shortlist of candidates and invite them for an interview. You should be present, as should the programme controller. You should look for the following qualities:

- a good voice
- an easygoing adaptable personality
- evidence of professional skills
- training in the basics of law and public administration
- experience of, or at least an interest in, the technicalities of radio
- local knowledge

Overall it is important to recruit the person with whom you feel you can best work. You are going to have to work together as a tight team. You need someone who is dependable and will work hard and whose skills complement your own. They need to have a good deal of common sense and a healthy attitude.

If they have no experience of radio, they need to be trained in the rudiments quickly. Ideally, send them for work experience to a working station or get them booked on one of the basic skills radio training courses.

Getting ready for the first day

There are innumerable jobs to be done simultaneously in readiness for the first day's bulletin.

Apart from making contacts and creating files, you should start looking for potential stories and getting interviews 'in the can'. Try to assemble a list of potential stories as you make contacts. Ask each contact what he or she sees as the biggest local issue. Read the local newspapers thoroughly. Use the run-up to on-air as the opportunity to gather as much material as possible. Remember this is a comparative luxury. After the station goes on the air, you will be responsible for putting out hourly news bulletins and will just not have the time to rush around everywhere recording interviews and talking to people in depth. Then you will be relying on the quality of the contacts you have built up during this period.

You also need to be discussing with the programme controller the quantity of news to be broadcasting each day. Should there be a bulletin each hour when the station is staffed by a journalist? Or should that journalist be responsible for gathering material for the following day? It is obviously important for the main news bulletins to be programmed hourly during breakfast time when the biggest audience is available. But should you have half-hour headlines or updates every 20 minutes? These are questions which need to be answered in talks with the programmers and balanced against the resources and staff you have available.

The first bulletin – getting an exclusive

During the run-up, aim to get a number of 'exclusives' ready for the first few days of broadcasting. Bear in mind that a lot of listeners will be trying the station out on its first few days, so it is important to make as big an impact as possible. Look for new angles on long-running local sagas; persuade a local VIP to comment on something he or she feels strongly about; find out about new developments or plans for the area. The criteria for these exclusives should be to find a story which affects your listeners directly or something about which they will have strong feelings. Remember to keep one exclusive for launch day and two others for days two and three.

Resource management

The problem of running any newsroom is that it is expensive. As far as many senior managers in Independent Radio are concerned, it is seen as an expensive necessity. They have to balance the need to provide a news service to their listeners with the fact that news spends money but rarely brings it in.

Working with a budget

As a news editor, you will be given a working budget. You are responsible for estimating your own costs. If you agree the budget, it is important to work within it. The budget you are given will probably be an annual figure. Break this down into a monthly sum, and divide it up among all the key areas of expenditure (Figure 10.3). Keep a careful record of all expenditure, especially invoices for freelance copy. Suitable headings for budget expenditure include: salaries, freelance cover, agency copy, staff expenses, mileage, entertainment, telephone and stationery.

Estimating costs

Always try to work out your budget for the year ahead based upon your actual expenditure last year. Study the figures carefully to see where you have overspent and underspent and adjust your estimates accordingly. Be realistic. In a situation

Radio Local News – 1992/93 Budget Submission*

1. News Agency Copy (monthly)

Miles News Agency	30 stories @ £6.36	£ 190.80
Wheeler's Press Agency	15 stories @ £6.36	£ 95.40
Ward News Agency	20 stories @ £6.36	£ 127.20
Abbott's Agency (court copy)	Fixed fee	£ 180.00
	Monthly Agency Total	£ 593.40

2. Freelance Journalist Cover (monthly)

Weekend Cover: 8 weekend (Sat/Sun) shifts (or replacement for staffer) @ £60 a day		£ 480.00
Holiday Cover: 12 staff × 4 weeks' annual leave = 48 weeks to cover. 4 weeks per month @ £300 per week (£60 a day)		£1200.00
	Monthly Freelance Total	£1680.00

2. Expenses (monthly)

4 reporters out on road 5 days a week. Average 10 miles a day @ 30p per mile = £15 a week each. Therefore £60 × 4 weeks		£ 240.00
Parking and miscellaneous		£ 50.00
	Monthly Expenses Total	£ 290.00

4. Sundries (monthly)

Public Relations/Entertainment		£ 30.00
Training		£ 50.00
Contingency (Elections, Major Incidents)		£ 250.00
	Monthly Sundries Total	£ 330.00

TOTAL MONTHLY NEWSROOM BUDGET (excluding salaries)

News Agency Copy	£ 593.40
Freelance Cover	£1680.00
Expenses	£ 290.00
Sundries	£ 330.00
Total Monthly	£2893.40

ANNUAL NEWSROOM RUNNING COSTS

£2893.40 × 12 = £34,720.80

*This budget excludes salaries and assumes that allowances for telephones, tapes, newspapers, National Insurance, stationery, depreciation, etc., are allocated to central departments.

Figure 10.3 A typical budget submission.

where you have to barter for your budget (almost always) with other departments, make sure you add a suitable 'mark-up' to your bid and be prepared to justify your expenditure under each of the headings above. Allow for inflation and give yourself the flexibility to act within budget. If anything, over-estimate.

Cutting costs and creating 'cosmetics'

You may be required to cut costs for a variety of reasons. For instance, it may be because you have overspent your originally agreed budget or that the commercial environment means that cuts are required in all departments of the radio station. Do not panic. First, try to limit the damage by making sure there is no unnecessary expenditure on copy from agencies or mileage incurred.

If the situation gets really bad, you will have to consider cutting costs drastically. However, your primary concern must be to protect the output of your newsroom as far as possible. Your aim must be to see through the crisis while creating the cosmetic impression on the air that the service is normal. This means the bulletins should continue unchanged as far as possible.

Here are some suggestions for gradual cost cutting:

- Cut freelance agency copy, especially the coverage of those court cases which are less important.
- Cut all mileage for face-to-face interviews. Only go out on stories when there is the chance of good audio and background sound. Do not just go to do an interview 'in a quiet corner somewhere'. Do phone interviews or, better still, get more interviewees to visit the studio.
- Do not use freelance journalists at all. Cover the shifts with staff.
- Reduce the use of unnecessary stationery. Review your use of expensive copy paper. Do not buy extravagant items like high-quality pens.
- Reduce the use of the phone until 1 pm. Obviously, important check calls need to be done, but it is usually possible to reschedule the use of the phone, especially for setting up overnight stories.

Chiltern Radio Network News Rota

MAR 11TH – 17TH		Monday 11th	Tuesday 12th	Wednesday 13th	Thursday 14th	Friday 15th	Saturday 16th	Sunday 17th
Network	News							
Support	News	Geoff	Geoff	Geoff	Geoff	Geoff.		
Unit:	Sport	Mike	Mike		Mike	Mike	Mike.	
Dunstable:								
5–1		Bill	Bill	Bill	Bill	Bill	Sheila	Doug
10–6		Sheila	Sheila	Sheila	Sheila	Sheila		
Bedford:								
5–1		Ron	Ron	Ron	Ron	Ron		
10–6		Tim	Tim	Tim	Tim	Tim		
Cambridge: 10–6		Kate	Kate	Kate	Kate	Kate		
Northampton: 10–6		Nick	Nick	Nick	Nick	Nick		
5–1		Dave	Dave	Dave	Dave	Dave		
11–7		Cathy	Cathy	Cathy	Cathy	Cathy		
Milton Keynes:								
5–1		Rich	Rich	Rich	Rich	Rich		
10–6		Corinna	Corinna	Corinna	Corinna	Corinna		

Figure 10.4 A newsroom rota for several sites.

Rotas

In a simple news operation, rotas are easy. The bigger the news operation, the harder rotas become (Figure 10.4). Do not forget to allow everyone the opportunity for variety within their job. Also allow for holidays and days off in lieu when people work at weekends. Try to keep people on the same shift throughout the week. It is dispiriting to have to work an early for two days to be followed by the rest of the week on a late. Be aware of individual preferences, but in the end you have the final say and make the decisions.

Dealing with complaints

No matter how careful you are, mistakes sometimes get through. Most of us do not like saying we are wrong, let alone admitting it publically by broadcasting a correction. There are some specific steps in dealing with complaints from listeners.

Phoned complaints

People who phone to complain can either be abusive or polite. Whatever their attitude, you should remain calm and courteous. First ask for a name, address and telephone number. If they have a genuine complaint, they will not object. If the complaint is unjustified or minor, this will discourage them. Then let the listener explain fully why they are upset. Try not to interrupt, take notes and do not go on the defensive. The best advice is to say you will investigate and call them back. Act rather than react.

Admitting and correcting an error

Check that a mistake really has been made. There are a surprising number of complaints made on the basis of something which has been misheard. Check the clip-up file or the logger tape (a slow-speed recording which has been made of the station's output and which is kept for three months or more).

If you are at fault, apologize and try to smooth ruffled feelings. Never put the blame somewhere else. If the inaccurate report came from a press agency, you simply say the report came from an experienced journalist in good faith. It is difficult to decide on action other than saying sorry privately. Sometimes, a listener will demand an apology. If you are wrong, you should say so, but on air corrections and apologies will be rare and sanctioned only by a senior member of staff.

Remember, listeners will in general have greater respect for you if you admit your mistakes and do not try to hide them.

Solicitors' letters

Do not panic if you receive a solicitor's letter about a story you have broadcast. However, never ignore it.

Usually it will request a transcript of a broadcast. It is up to you whether or not you supply this transcript. In the end, you can be forced to do so. The best advice when dealing with solicitors is to use your own legal advisers. Although this will be expensive, it is nevertheless important to make sure your legal dealings are correct and everything is done 'by the book'. Your solicitor will advise you what to admit, if anything. If you reply to a solicitor's letter on your own, be sure to include the words 'Without Prejudice'. This means your letter is legally off-the-record. Make sure your company is covered by specific insurance which is available, in case you are taken to court for libel or contempt.

In the BBC, you have access to 24-hour-a-day legal advice through the corporation's lawyers. A check with a duty solicitor is, of course, free to BBC journalists.

Dealing with regulatory authorities

The three main regulatory authorities you will have to deal with are the Radio Authority (in Independent Radio), the Broadcasting Complaints Commission and the Broadcasting Standards Council.

The Radio Authority requires stations to keep recordings of broadcasts for 42 days. It will investigate complaints about

CHANTLER, HARRIS & CO.
SOLICITORS AND COMMISSIONERS FOR OATHS

BANK CHAMBERS, 14 TAVISTOCK STREET
CANNING, SOMERSET CG1 4ER
TELEPHONE CANNING 23908 (5 LINES)
FACSIMILE CANNING 33618

The News Editor
Wessex Radio Limited
Tolworth Cross
Canning
CG2 4RR

14th June 1991
Our ref. MBW/AG

Dear Sir,

re Wessex Radio News, 1st June 1991

We are instructed by Mr. John Doe, Managing Director of AB Engineering Limited, Priorswood, Canning, concerning an interview broadcast on the above programme with Mr. Richard Roe, Chief Shop Steward of the Associated Operators Union.

You are of course aware that there is currently a dispute between our client's Employer Company and the Associated Operators Union. We are instructed that the following words of Mr. Roe, quoted verbatim, were broadcast by yourselves: "The real problem is that the management of ABE are incompetent. I don't think the managing director could measure a piece of string and get the right answer. They can't manage anything, and they don't know much about engineering either, for what I can see.".

Your legal advisors must surely have informed you that the dissemination of such a statement by Wessex Radio is defamatory of our client and we are instructed to seek damages in libel from yourself for its broadcast.

Since it took place our client has found difficulty in the business community in handling the affairs of the company due to the wholly unjustified attack of Mr. Roe broadcast by yourselves.

We enclose a form of apology which we require to be broadcast on the same programme within seven days of today at a point in the programme commensurately prominent to the original broadcast. Please advise us by return when the broadcast will take place.

Furthermore, unless we receive written confirmation within seven days of your preparedness to pay a reasonable sum in damages for your libel against our client, a writ seeking damages, together with a claim for interest and costs, will be issued without further reference to yourselves.

We look forward to hearing from you within the time limits specified.

Yours faithfully,

for Chantler, Harris & Co.

GEORGE BURROWS, STEPHEN BURROWS, MICHAEL WOOLACOTT LL.B., JULIAN RUNDLE

THIS FIRM IS REGULATED BY THE LAW SOCIETY FOR INVESTMENT BUSINESS

Figure 10.5 A (fictitious) solicitor's letter alleging libel. Always use your legal advisers to reply.

inaccuracy, bias and offensiveness, taking action if necessary. It can admonish the company, request a broadcast apology or correction, and also impose a penalty which can include a warning, a fine and the shortening or revocation of a licence.

The Broadcasting Complaints Commission deals with complaints from those who feel they have been unfairly treated or had their privacy invaded. After adjudication, the Commission may require the publication of its findings.

The Broadcasting Standards Council considers complaints about violence, sexual conduct and taste and decency in programmes and advertisements. After adjudication, the Council may require publication of its findings.

Making news an audience winner

News has to be seen in the context of the programming of the radio station as a whole. There is no point in broadcasting news if nobody is listening. It is therefore the job of the newsroom as well as the programmers to win audiences.

Targeting audiences

Some news editors believe that they not only have to consider radio's traditional advantages over other media as a source of news, but take this a step further by targeting stories to specific groups of listeners.

They consider the format of the station when making decisions about what stories to cover. For instance, a Top 40 music station can have stories about pop personalities in its news to make it relevant. A black music station needs stories about the black community. An oldies station needs stories about Frank Sinatra and other singers. After all, people listen to music stations mainly for the music. It is your job to tell them what is going on with specific reference to their interests. The one way their interest can be identified is the fact they are tuned into your station and the music it is playing.

Take careful note of the audience statistics and demographic breakdown of the listenership. This will give you clues as to the sort of stories you can usefully cover. The key advice is *make your stories relevant*.

Different formats

There are many different formats for presenting news on the radio. The most traditional is the top-of-the-hour news bulletins. Some stations, though, prefer news at half-past the hour. Their reasoning is that their rivals carry news on the top of the hour and if they are playing music then, they have a chance of picking up any listeners who may tune out because of a news bulletin.

Rolling news is also a popular format. This means there are constant news updates throughout the clock hour, either read by the presenter or DJ or newsreader. BBC Local Radio is now required to have 70% speech or more on its daily output and broadcasts extended news bulletins as well as news and topical features.

Other formats becoming more popular include the 'double header', with a DJ and a newsreader co-presenting a programme which takes in music as well as an informal, chatty look at the news. Live interviews can also be accommodated easily into this format.

Presentation styles

Make the style and sound of your news bulletins or programmes match the radio station style as a whole. It is no use having BBC World Service style presentation on a Top 40 music station or visa versa. Think of the listener and what he or she wants. Whatever style of presentation you choose, the important thing is to make sure your bulletins are authoritative and believable.

Sponsorship – the dangers and delights

Sponsorship of news is not allowed in British commercial radio. This is because of a fear that editorial independence could be compromised. For example, if your sponsor was a chemicals firm it might be difficult to do a story criticizing that firm.

However, news is an expensive business and there are arguments which say it would help if news is sponsored just like other parts of the radio station's output, such as the travel news and weather. There is no shortage of companies willing to have their name associated with a news bulletin because of the authority that it conveys. Indeed, Independent Radio stations carry Newslink commercials in the morning and evening peak bulletins. These are ordinary commercials juxtaposed to the news bulletin. In this way, IR stations do not currently have to pay a fee for IRN's service.

Perhaps in the future more direct sponsorship will be allowed, easing the burden of financing news-gathering for small stations. However, it will be vitally important to maintain the editorial integrity of the news and ensure there are guarantees of editorial independence. Existing advertisers are unable to influence a story which criticizes them or brings them bad publicity and future sponsors must surely agree to similar controls.

11

Specialist programmes

The news round-up

The news round-up programme is different from a bulletin in that it may use older stories and also longer versions of stories.

Older stories means by hours, not days. A news programme at, say, 5 pm may well include anything from that day's events that is worth having and is still current or can be made current. Many listeners will have heard nothing since they left for work at 8.30 am.

Presentation of these programmes will be different too. For example, they can be 'double-headed' – in other words, using two presenters. The style can be less formal, even chatty, and there may well be 'guest appearances' from other people giving travel reports or financial news.

A typical format

Here is a fictional, but typical, format for an evening news programme on a commercial station, anchored by two presenters:

17:00:00 Opening signature tune, under headlines JOHN
00:30 Teasers JOHN
01:00 News bulletin PETER
05:00 Travel – AA Roadwatch reporter
05:45 Travel – trains and planes JOHN

06:30 BREAK 1
09:00 First long audio CUED BY PETER
11:00 Second long audio CUED BY JOHN
13:00 BREAK 2
15:00 Headlines PETER
16:00 Financial report – bank reporter
18:00 Third long audio CUED BY JOHN
21:00 Sport MICHAEL
25:00 BREAK 3
27:00 Fourth long audio (1′30″ max) CUED BY JOHN
28:30 Headlines PETER (PREFADE SIG. AT 29:00)
29:20 Closing sequence PETER and JOHN
29:59 Signature tune out

This type of programme is designed for an evening audience who may well be driving home and dipping in and out every few minutes. You would not have to hear the whole programme to get a reasonable idea of the day's main news stories and you would probably hear at least one in depth.

The note to 'prefade' the signature tune at 29:00 means that the music will run from 29:00 to 29:59. It can be faded up at any time and still end neatly on schedule. This is the job of the producer, technical operator or studio manager, if used.

A programme like this is not generally driven by the presenters because they do not have enough time to check that everything is ready, including the three 'guest' reporters and the commercial breaks, as well as present the programme.

Since this schedule is fairly tight, in reality the fourth long audio would probably be an expendable item. One and a half minutes can easily be absorbed by a couple of extra commercials or an overrun by the financial or sport presenter.

Jingles

Jingles and idents (identity music 'stabs') play an important part in keeping a programme like this moving. There will be separate versions of the signature tune for start and finish and probably several short versions which are recognizably part of the same piece, maybe just 3–10 seconds long. These can be played at intervals during the programme, such as around the headlines sequence, to maintain continuity and remind the listener what the programme is all about.

Features and documentaries

Feature pieces are a chance to tell a story in more depth. A package or wrap consists of at least one clip of audio, which is linked by a reporter to make a complete story. A package is, in effect, a voicer with some audio inserted into it. A news package may run 35 seconds or so, with just one piece of audio: at the other extreme is the news documentary, which may run for an hour and have dozens of clips in it.

In each case, the basic principles are the same. Audio should add to the story, not just repeat what the reporter has just said. Each link into each clip can be treated like a separate news cue, except that the opening line of each cue does not, of course, start the story from scratch. Each cue should move the overall story on in some way by expanding an earlier part or contradicting it.

The pieces of long audio mentioned in the previous section on news round-up programmes may well be packages. The great advantage of a package is that, by using appropriate audio,both sides of an argument can be aired in the same piece. Often, conflicting views have greater impact if they are heard in quick succession by the listener.

Another point to note is that longer packages can be far more creative, using sound effects and music as well as recordings of speech.

The essence of a documentary

Here is the beginning of a fictitious documentary about British Rail:

> FX: Bristol Temple Meads station. Atmosphere at 0500. Down and under . . .
>
> REPORTER: Temple Meads station, Bristol, at five in the morning. Most of the city is fast asleep, but Temple Meads never sleeps. Even at Christmas there are still people on duty, even though no trains run for the public. The area manager is Paul Robinson . . .
>
> AUDIO (ROBINSON): In: 'We can never close a station . . .' Out: '. . . day or night, we are here.'

FX: station. Down and under . . .

REPORTER: Every day, thousands of people use Temple Meads. To deal with them, there are staff like Leading Railman Jack Clark . . .

AUDIO (CLARK): In: 'My father joined the Great Western . . .'

The radio documentary must have a shape and a story to tell. You, as producer, must know whether it will have a definite conclusion to reach, or whether it is a series of individual pictures in sound, put together because they are more effective in a single frame. Remember that other people's words are often more effective than your own, and that there are many sounds other than words. Use all these resources and your documentary will be memorable.

Setting up the documentary

The making of a documentary is hard work. On a local radio station it may be a single-handed job. If you need to interview perhaps 20 people, that means 20 separate appointments to be made and kept. Try not to get too much audio from each one. If you record half-hour interviews, that adds up to 10 hours of continuous speech to assess later! Editing can be tremendously time consuming on this scale. So rationalize your efforts at the start. If you will want at the most one minute from each person in the finished production, 10 interview minutes on tape should be enough unless they turn out to be unexpectedly fascinating.

Make sure that you have access to the music and sound effects you need. Is your documentary one of a series? If so, does the series have a distinctive house style – a standard beginning and end with its own signature tune? Any standard introduction will have to be accommodated in your particular piece.

Editing the finished programme

Be ruthless when you edit your documentary. It is a common mistake to include too much. A one-hour documentary on a commercial station is actually 48 minutes; the other 12 minutes are taken up by commercial breaks and the hourly news. In those 48 minutes, you will do well to include more than about 35 minutes of audio, unless your own contributions are very brief.

Look for voices and sounds that are startling and consider one to end the programme. Go out on a bang, if that is appropriate to your subject. Make the listener listen by the force of your material and do not let it sag. If something seems rather boring, leave it out. Keep the pace moving and use shorter rather than longer clips of audio.

Finally, a complete programme must be recorded in good time before transmission. Do not forget to book a studio and anyone needed to drive the audio inserts while you record the links between each one. Or you can self-op as you would a bulletin. If possible, allow some time between the master recording and the transmission date. Editing documentaries on the day of transmission is not unknown, but work done in a hurry may not be your best.

Outside broadcasts

Planning an outside broadcast (OB) is like planning a battle. You must have everyone in the right place at the right time with the right equipment.

Many of the difficulties encountered on outside broadcasts are technical rather than personal. The hospital to be visited by royalty next week will turn out to be in a low part of the area where radio links are not effective. This means either a landline or driving to nearby high ground with freshly recorded material and transmitting it from there.

Generally, outside broadcasts must be planned ahead as far as possible – preferably at least a month. For example, deciding to cover a Royal Visit the day before will be pointless – in practice, a reporter is unlikely to be allowed anywhere near without the precious 'Royal Rota' pass issued by the Central Office of Information. You must apply for these passes well in advance.

There are several ways of getting information back from an outside broadcast:

- landline
- broadcast link

- telephone link
- courier

Each has its own advantages and problems.

Landlines

Landlines must be booked in advance with the telecommunications company. They are not cheap. They will usually tie your OB team to one spot, except for roving personnel who can either move nearby with a long microphone lead or further away with a portable tape recorder. If recorders are used, is the material to be played back to base straight away? If so, remember that material played down the landline will either go straight to air or the OB must be replaced by studio output during the playback of material from site (Figure 11.1).

Broadcast links

The broadcast link from the station radio car uses a frequency well outside that available on domestic radio receivers, but it can

Figure 11.1 Northants Radio roadshow – an example of the lighter side of outside broadcasts.

be heard by anyone with the right equipment; it is not, therefore, watertight. Anything sent back in this way is being broadcast, even if not through your studio on the normal frequency. Such a link is also vulnerable to the failures of aerials or transmitter. It may be useless in some kinds of situations, such as low ground or areas well screened by buildings or trees.

If radio links are to be used, a field test in advance is essential. On the day, other electrical equipment could cause interference. Beware.

Telephone links

The telephone provides only low-quality output, adequate for a reporter's voicer but not much else. There can also be problems with actually finding a telephone when all the nearby callboxes are likely to be in heavy demand by other reporters. Sometimes a friendly householder will help. Mobile phones offer some considerable advantages, but at the scene of a major disaster the police can (and do) ask British Telecom to restrict the use of mobile phones to authorized users only – which usually means just the emergency services. Similar restrictions might be in force for security reasons during VIP visits.

Couriers

Using a courier to bring tape back to base means that all semblance of a live outside broadcast is lost. There is no chance of reacting to sudden developments at the OB site. Coverage restricted to a courier service is not really an outside broadcast at all.

To summarize, OBs need to be carefully thought out, well ahead. It is likely that at least two of the communication methods outlined above will have some part to play. One more element is also crucial – the availability of a standby programme back at base to cover emergency breakdowns.

The phone-in

For many years, the phone-in programme has been the staple diet of local radio. Critics say it is no more than a cheap way of filling air time, but phone-ins can be provocative, interesting and useful. What determines the success of a phone-in is the way it is put together and planned.

Selecting the subject

There are a number of types of phone-ins which include:

- an 'open-line' discussion
- an advice line with a guest such as a doctor or lawyer
- a topical discussion on one particular subject with a guest

When planning an open-line or topical discussion, the best source of material is undoubtedly daily newspapers. These often provide the spur to which the listener can relate.

Studio operation on the air

It is possible for the presenter to take calls off-air and 'line them up' while a record is playing, if the phone-in consists of music as well as calls. However, the best way of running a phone-in is to have the calls 'screened' or answered by an assistant.

The assistant needs to write down the caller's name, the area from where they are calling and a phone number (for reference). The caller is then put on hold and the details passed to the presenter, either on paper or by means of a visual talkback unit, such as a personal computer and VDU.

Before the caller goes on the air, he or she also needs to be told to turn their radio down to avoid 'howl round' or feedback or the effects of an electronic delay (see below). The assistant also needs to make sure the caller is sensible, with a legitimate question or point.

Another way of running a phone-in is to invite calls before the programme starts, take callers' phone numbers and call them back while on the air. This gives you more control over the editorial development of the programme.

Figures 11.2 and 11.3 show a control room and a well-equipped studio desk, respectively.

Figure 11.2 A control room at BBC Ulster (Courtesy of Tim Arnold).

Figure 11.3 A well-equipped studio desk at BBC Ulster (Courtesy of Tim Arnold).

The presenter

Phone-in presenters need to be fluent, witty, wise, provocative and occasionally rude. They need to be positive and stimulate conversation which often means playing devil's advocate. It goes without saying they need to be quick-thinking, alert to defamatory comments and sufficiently democratic to let all callers put their point of view.

The delay

Some stations insist on an electronic delay device on phone-ins. This means that the whole programme is shifted in time for between seven and 10 seconds via a special tape recorder or digital device. The reason is that if someone says something defamatory or obscene, this can be deleted a few seconds before transmission and the delayed recording can be replaced by the live output.

Problem phone-ins

You need great sensitivity to handle a problem phone-in, which can be accused of being exploitative and the aural equivalent of voyeurism. It is a great responsibility and has to be taken seriously.

You need expert guests, such as psychiatrists, doctors and lawyers to handle the calls about sexual and relationship problems, medical conditions and legal queries. Remember, the callers are using the radio station as a friend who can give specialist unbiased personal advice. During this type of phone-in, you are no longer 'broadcasting' but 'narrowcasting' and talking to the individual, hoping other listeners – who might never pluck up the courage to phone – can identify with the particular problem being discussed.

The music–speech mix

The local radio programme which mixes both speech and music is probably one of the most difficult to do well. It is the ultimate test of the all-round broadcaster, combining the music skills of the DJ with the skills of the journalist. It is hard work but can be highly rewarding.

Qualities of the presenter

The presenter needs to be at home handling music, interviews, script-reading and technical operation. In addition, a logical, well-organized mind with the ability to think quickly and react to what is happening is required. A good working knowledge of current affairs and the ability to ad-lib rather than simply relying on scripts is an asset, as is the ability to talk to time. In short, you need to be able to cope with anything and everything. In general, it is easier for a journalist to adapt to becoming a music presenter than the other way round.

Getting the balance right

In most programmes it is necessary to make sure there is not too much speech or too much music. The exact proportion will be defined by the station policy; for instance, BBC local radio stations have a policy of no less than 70% speech at peak listening times.

Arguably the safest rule for mixing music and speech is to limit speech items to no more than four minutes, the average length of a record. This means listeners are likely to stay tuned through something in which they are not interested simply because they know it will not last long and something more appealing may be following. An interview with a celebrity, for example, could be spread out in three four-minute sections with records in between, rather than one 12-minute block.

Music selection is particularly important in programmes which have a speech content. All the music must be recognizable and popular, for example all top-five hits, to prevent the listener tuning out because they do not recognize something. Listeners are remarkably tolerant of music they do not like which has been a hit simply because it is familiar.

The idea is to keep the listener listening for as long as possible. You need constantly to promote what is coming up in the programme, including features, interviews and music. However it helps to *be specific* about what you are promoting, e.g. a particular record or a specific person to be interviewed.

Blending speech and music

The programme is likely to consist of tapes, carts, live interviews, links to the radio car, links to outside studios, telephone interviews, a phone-in element, traffic and travel news, sports news and, of course, music. It requires the highest standards of professionalism to link all these elements together slickly.

The key to all this is preparation and being well organized. Before going on air, everything needs to be sorted out so you know exactly what you are going to use and when you are going to use it. Interview introductions need to have been scripted and a few questions prepared in advance in case there is a distracting panic before the actual live interview. When you are on the air, you need to be thinking about five or 10 minutes ahead of yourself to make sure the next item is all ready to go. You should always have a record or CD cued up in case of emergencies.

If you are creating a new programme, the best advice is not to be too ambitious at first. Start small and build up the content gradually as you become more adept at handling the technical and editorial complexity of the programme.

Try to develop the skill of voicing over the introductions of records and CDs. It is, of course, important you do not talk over the vocals. Most DJs find they can do this after a while through instinct, although you might need to use a stopwatch or timer at first. The effect of this is that it helps to blur the edges between the music and speech and prevent the 'stop–start' type of presentation which sounds so dated.

Elections

Elections make good radio. There is the buzz of the count, the excited claims of rival candidates and the dramatic moment when the Acting Returning Officer reveals the result.

But the law takes a stern view of anyone who prejudices the fairness of an election. You must be sure that your radio station does not let enthusiasm overtake prudence and that you follow the rules. There is a timetable which lays down what may and must not be done, rather like the progress of a court case.

As soon as an election is announced, this timetable takes shape. We will deal here with General Elections, although the rules for local elections are similar as far as media coverage is concerned.

Announcement of election

From the moment when the election is announced, Parliament is dissolved and until nominations close you would be wise to steer clear of all potential candidates. If they are allowed to broadcast about constituency matters in this period, they (and you) are breaking the law.

Closing of nominations

This is the first important stage when all would-be candidates must make sure they have been validly nominated to the local Acting Returning Officer. At this stage all 'prospective parliamentary candidates' cease to be prospective. From now on you must observe the rules of balance.

We will assume there are four candidates for the fictional constituency of Canning West. From the close of nominations, each candidate for Canning West must have equal airtime. 'Equal' can, of course, include none. But if you interview the Conservative candidate Michael Blue, you must give the same time to the other three – not necessarily on the same occasion, but overall. This means *all* airtime, including the clip recorded for news which has not yet gone out.

If 25 seconds of Mr Blue is broadcast after the close of nominations, even if it is recorded beforehand, you must provide 25 seconds, as near as possible, with the other three. If you do not, they could report you to the Acting Returning Officer for Canning who could prosecute (although a warning and a request to restore the balance is more likely). If you allow candidates airtime at all during an election period (and there is no law which says you must), it is wise to keep a log in the newsroom to be brought up to date after every bulletin.

Discussion programmes

You may have the idea of getting all four candidates round a studio table for a live discussion in this period. On the face of it, this is fine. But take care. If all four turn up, they must get equal time during the programme as far as possible. The law is reasonable on this point, and the chairman of a live discussion is not expected to use a stopwatch. But there must be no glaring discrepancy. It is very important that all the main candidates agree in writing that they will attend for the broadcast. A refusal by one or more makes it unsafe to go ahead, because balance would be impossible. If one drops out at the last moment, it is reasonable to proceed, mentioning the absent candidate at least once or twice and explaining why he or she is unrepresented. The candidate might nominate someone else to stand in, and you should accept the chosen substitute. If, however, the last-minute absentee tries to stop the programme altogether, claiming legal rights, it would be wise to check with your solicitor before proceeding.

Practice during recent elections, if not the letter of the law, suggests that candidates from minor parties, if not present, should be mentioned by name and party during the programme. Although the person chairing the discussion should be impartial, that does not prevent the policies of absent candidates being put forward by the chair for discussion.

Day of the poll

The poll opens in a General Election at 7 am and ends at 10 pm. Local elections start an hour later and finish an hour earlier. During that time, you must not broadcast any political propaganda at all, even if balanced between all candidates in a constituency. News reports from 7 am must keep to the basic facts that the polls have opened, that it is a sunny day (or otherwise), that the turnout is predicted to be heavy, and other non-political issues. From 10 pm that night the field is wide open and all special restrictions end. But watch that no candidate (in an excess of enthusiasm) says anything about one of the others which could be libellous at any time. The law of defamation is not suspended in an election!

Commentaries

The commentary is the broadcaster's chance to paint pictures for the listener. In most cases, the event itself will be a 'diary' one, which will be known about in advance, and we will discuss that kind here. There is another type of commentary though – the completely unexpected moment when a news story breaks before your eyes and you have a microphone. As the rioters advance up the street, or as you watch an aircraft dive into the ground, you must literally make up what you say as you go along. There are very few pieces of advice which will come in useful then, except *keep talking*.

Planning a commentary

If you are to commentate at a major event, read all you can in advance. If the Queen is scheduled to meet the Sea Scouts, know the name of their commanding officer. If she will be greeted by the Lord Lieutenant of the county, make sure you know not merely his name but also why he received the DSO in 1942. It may come in handy. It is no accident that, during great national events, the commentators always have something to say. It is rare for a hold-up to occur with Coronations and other ceremonial occasions, but when one does happen you discover how much research the commentator has done: '. . . and as we wait for the Royal Coach to start moving again from where it has stopped in front of the statue, it might be appropriate to mention that one of the first television outside broadcasts ever, the Coronation of King George the Sixth in 1937, also used the plinth of the same statue to place one of those early black-and-white cameras which were developed by a team at EMI in Hayes . . .' and so on. Much of your research will never be heard, but you will be comforted, on the day, that you have a reservoir of material which you will have reduced, naturally, into easily read notes in front of you.

Also make sure, by a visit in advance, that *you* will see what is going on! It will be very embarrassing to admit that your view has been blocked by a new bandstand which was put up overnight. Speak at length with the organizers. Make sure they know you will be there on the day and why.

Communicating mood

Great occasions can be happy or sad, and it is up to the radio commentator to convey the general emotion by tone or voice. Describing the Lord Mayor's Show is not the same as describing a Remembrance Day ceremony. Be sensitive about the type of event you are covering. Nobody wants you to be a ham actor, but there are shades of emotion which you should properly use.

Content and style

What you say will depend on the opportunities you are given. it may be that you are called on to provide several two-minute pieces into another programme. There is no time, then, for long reminiscences about where they put TV cameras in 1937. On the other hand, you could be carrying the programme for much longer. Then, more detail is essential.

Whatever else you leave out, do not forget to describe the clothing of female Royalty in as much detail as you reasonably can. Many listeners are fascinated by what colours the princess has chosen for her spring collection. If male Royalty wears anything other than the usual lounge suit (maybe a kilt?), then of course that should be mentioned too.

Silence, please . . .

When you are facing a microphone which is callously live for a long period, you may feel a temptation to fill every second. Resist it. However golden your tones, the listener would like a rest from them now and then. Remember that the sounds of the day itself are also available to tell their own story. Pause for a few seconds as the prince gets out of the car; let the sound of the platoon coming smartly to attention speak for itself. Your words are no substitute for the unmistakable 'thwack' of dozens of army boots all hitting the ground at precisely the same moment. If you provide the frame, the listeners will be able to see the picture for themselves.

Sport

The essence of a successful sports programme is simple – supplying a fast, accurate and instant service of information. A whole book could be written about sports reporting and presenting, but here are a few hints and tips.

Match reports

Match reports are a bonus, and coverage of major events such as league soccer are governed by national contracts. The listener wants to know instantly that Bryan Robson has equalized for Manchester United at Liverpool, for example. This is the crucial news. A reporter can add more details a few minutes later.

For many years the coverage of football has been governed by national agreements allowing a specified number of 30-second reports in each half, plus preview, half-time and full-time updates. The general rule is to keep your reports simple and factual. Over-elaboration confuses the listener.

The main difference between TV and radio sports reporting is that on radio you are the link, whereas on TV you are the missing link. In other words, the audience can turn the voice off on TV and still follow what is going on. On radio, you are the only link with the action.

Figure 11.4 gives a selection of well-worn sporting clichés for the sports reporter to avoid.

Daily sports bulletins

A successful radio sports operation's credibility is also dependent on the quality of the daily sports bulletins, which should be authoritative and informative. The guidelines to writing sports copy are the same as for news. The key to success is to establish good relations with your contacts such as football managers or rugby coaches. To fill a sports bulletin, you have to start from scratch. You cannot rely on police calls like the newsdesk. Here are a few hints:

They've sprung the offside trap	He buried the cross from six yards
The goalkeeper hasn't been getting his knees dirty	He hit the ball well wide of the post
A classic match of two halves	His telescopic sight needs urgent repair
The strikers have been firing blanks all day	He headed it nowhere in particular
The visitors' defence pressed the self-destruct button	The manager must have wished he'd stayed in bed
The goalkeeper has so little to do, he is in danger of frostbite	He's going to take an early bath
He slammed the ball into the back of the net	

Figure 11.4 Well-worn sporting clichés to be avoided.

1. Be courteous.
2. Be certain of your facts before you do an interview. Managers have been known to walk away from hapless radio interviewers who have asked, 'So who are you playing tomorrow?'
3. Stick to the facts. Do not be misled by wild speculation, however tempting.

The sports diary

A successful sports desk is based on one thing – the proper and effective use of a diary. All the fixtures should be entered, but notes should be made of follow-up stories. For example, on Monday the 1st you run a story with a local team manager saying Smith is out of action for three weeks with a hamstring injury. Then, immediately, you enter the story for the 21st and put it to the manager again. Not only will that show the manager that you are on top of things, but it will also create a similar impression with the listener.

12

The future of radio news

The future of radio news is assured. In the 1990s there will be more local radio stations and therefore more jobs for journalists. It is a real growth industry. There will always be an appetite for local news.

However, there will be changes in the way newsrooms are run. They will operate with fewer people and those people will be required to have the all-round skills of the experienced broadcaster. It is an exciting and challenging time to be involved in local radio news.

There will always be a need to attract and keep audiences. In commercial radio, it is this ability to win audiences which attracts advertisers and therefore provides the money to keep the news machine rolling. It is no different from the way national and local newspapers operate. The essential thing is to remain impartial and independent, not bowing to any pressure exerted by advertisers or sponsors. This would sound the death knell for local radio news and break the bond of trust which exists between broadcaster and listener.

Although there will always be a place for the 'tell it straight' type of radio journalism, we will begin to see a greater emphasis on production and presentation values in radio news, again in the quest for audiences. This, of course, needs to be tempered with a constant vigilance for the quality of content. Good writing and snappy presentation is all well and good, as long as what you are writing about is interesting, relevant and accurate.

Technically there will be a revolution in the nineties. More and more newsrooms will become computerized. The aim will be a cart-less and paper-less newsroom. News bulletins will be written, compiled and timed on-screen. Audio will be stored on hard disk. The newsreader will sit in front of a VDU to deliver the bulletin, reading the script and cues off-screen and touching the screen to activate audio cuts and clips.

The technical revolution will extend to the reporter on the ground as well as the newsroom and newsdesk. More and more use will be made of high-quality digital audio tape for recording audio and interviews. The equipment will become smaller and smaller, thus more portable. And the speed and quality of filing stories back to base will improve with the introduction of improved portable telephones. Reporters are already filing direct into the newsroom computer using portable word processors which can be linked up to phones. All this will enable reporters and newsdesk staff to do their job quicker and more efficiently, leaving more time to follow up other stories. Productivity will increase because the new technology will be increasingly seen as a 'liberator'.

With all the technical and operational changes, it is still important to remember the basics. There will always be a need for bright young talent in the industry. It is vital to keep these people within radio and not let them use radio simply as a stepping stone to TV. This can only be done by making radio exciting and profitable in which to work, with all the job satisfaction anyone could need.

However, there is a danger which needs guarding against, especially with the increased use of new technology in newsrooms. There could be a tendency to think of news as that which simply appears on the screen or the printer.

It must never be forgotten that news is that which you go out and find, through your own efforts.

Appendix

Useful addresses for radio courses

Full-time radio courses

BBC Journalist Training, Broadcasting House, London W1A 1AA

BBC Local Radio Training Unit, Grafton House, 379 Euston Road, London NW1 3AU

BBC World Service Training, Bush House, PO Box 76, Strand, London WC2B 4PH

Barnet College (Radio Journalism), Wood Street, Barnet, Hertfordshire EN5 4AZ

Birmingham Community Radio Training, Macro House, 180 Soho Hill, Birmingham B19 1AG

Centre for Journalism Studies (Radio Journalism), University of Wales, 69 Park Place, Cardiff CF1 3AS

Christ Church College (Radio, Film and TV Studies), North Holmes Road, Canterbury, Kent CT1 1OU

Darlington College of Technology (Radio Journalism), Cleveland Avenue, Darlington, Co Durham DL3 7BB

Falmouth School of Art and Design (Radio Journalism), Woodlane, Falmouth, Cornwall TR11 4RA

Handsworth Technical College (Radio Journalism), Handsworth Council House, Handsworth B21 9DP

Highbury College of Technology (Radio Journalism), Dovercourt Road, Cosham, Portsmouth PO6 2SA

Lancashire Polytechnic (Radio and TV Journalism), Preston, Lancashire PR1 2TO

London College of Printing (Radio Journalism), Elephant and Castle, London SE1 6SB
Longlands College of Further Education (Community Radio), Douglas Street, Middlesbrough, Cleveland TS4 2JW
Sutton Coldfield College, Lichfield Road, Sutton Coldfield, Birmingham B74 2NW

Short training courses for radio

Aircheck Ltd, Kelly House, Warwick Road, Tunbridge Wells, Kent TN1 1YL
Community Radio Association, 119 Southbank House, Black Prince Road, London SE1 7SJ
Media First, PO Box 2000, The Watershed, Cannon's Road, Bristol BS99 7SN
Radio Training Unit, Granville House, Granville Road, Leicester LE1 7RW

Degree courses relating to radio

Birmingham Polytechnic (Communication Studies), Perry Barr, Birmingham B42 2SU
Brighton Polytechnic (Communication Studies), Moulsecoomb, Brighton, East Sussex BN2 4AT
Bristol Polytechnic (Diploma in Broadcast Journalism), Coldharbour Lane, Frenchay, Bristal BS16 1QY
Coventry Polytechnic (Communication Studies), Priory Street, Coventry CV1 5FB
Dorset Institute (BA Hons Media Production), Wallisdown Road, Poole, Doreset BN12 5BB
Liverpool Polytechnic (Media and Cultural Studies), Rodney House, 70 Mount Pleasant, Liverpool L3 5UX
Middlesex Polytechnic (Communication Studies), Trent Park, Cockfosters Road, Barnet, London EN4 0PT
Newcastle-upon-Tyne Polytechnic (Media Production). Ellison Building, Ellison Place, Newcastle-upon-Tyne NE1 8ST
Norwich City College (Communication Studies), Ipswich Road, Norwich, Norfolk NR22 2LJ

Polytechnic of Wales (BA Media Studies), Llantwit Road, Treforest, Pontypridd, Mid Glamorgan CF37 1DL

Sunderland Polytechnic (Communication Studies), Langham Tower, Ryhope Road, Sunderland SR2 7EE

Trent Polytechnic (Communication Studies), Burton Street, Nottingham NG1 4BU

Trinity and All Saints College (Communication and Cultural Studies), Brownberrie Lane, Horsforth, Leeds LS18 5HD

University of London, Goldsmiths College (Media Studies), Lewisham Way, New Cross, London SE14 6NW

For a list of colleges which run City and Guilds Media Techniques courses, contact: City and Guilds Regional Advisory Council for Further Education, Tavistock House South, Tavistock Square, London WC1H 9LR.

Glossary

Actuality: A recording of someone speaking, or of an event, used in news bulletins or similar output. (Note: a reporter's voice-piece is not in itself actuality, neither is any recording made for fictional or dramatic purposes.)

Ad lib: Speaking without a script.

Archive (news): A file of old stories for reference. This can be copy, audio, or both.

Aircheck: A recording of a broadcaster or programme. Sometimes used for demonstration purposes.

Audio: Literally any sound, but frequently used in radio to mean a recording of speech or sound effects for output. Therefore a voice piece, cut or package are all audio.

Balancing unit: *See* TBU.

Bulk eraser: A device which generates a powerful magnetic field to erase tape.

cps: Centimetres per second (tape speed).

Cartridge ('cart'): An endless loop of tape enclosed in a plastic case. Inaudible tones are used to achieve automatic cueing. Used for short audio items, including news clips, commercials, trails and jingles.

Check calls: Routine telephone calls from a newsroom to the police, fire service, etc.

Clean tape: Tape which is either new or has had all previous recordings erased.

Clip (BBC): A piece of news audio: usually on cartridge.

Copy: Written material ready for broadcasting.

Copy story: A news story without audio.

Cue (1): The start point on a recording. ('This tape is cued' – this tape is ready to play.) Also, a start signal to a live speaker. ('I will cue Donald at the end of this record . . .')

Cue (2): The written introduction to a piece of audio, especially news.

Cut (IR): A piece of news audio: usually on cartridge.

Delay (also profanity D.): A device which inserts a time delay between studio and transmitter output, usually of seven seconds. Once in operation, a delay is not obvious to the listener, but the broadcaster can prevent the last seven seconds of studio output from reaching the transmitter by dropping back to 'real time'. This enables censoring of undesirable material on programmes such as public phone-ins.

Demo tape: A recording of a broadcaster (or would-be broadcaster) sent with a job application. Two or three minutes is usually plenty, and cassettes are customary.

Dirty tape. Tape which has not been fully erased. If a dirty cartridge is used for another recording, the previous signal will still be heard in the background.

Dubbing: Copying a recording on to another tape.

Editing: Changing a recording after it has been made, usually by removing part of it. Editing can be achieved by splicing the tape, or else by dubbing selected portions.

Equalization ('EQ'): Changing the frequency response of a device (that is, which types of sound it responds to most); usually a microphone. A voice may be improved (made deeper or crisper) by equalization, but EQ controls should only be adjusted by the experienced.

Fire: To start a piece of audio, especially on cartridge.

GTS: Greenwich Time Signal ('the pips').

ips: Inches per second (tape speed).

Incremental radio (IR): In the UK, an additional Independent radio station (usually fairly small) in an area which already has at least one commercial service.

Landline: A special cable link which can carry sound at full bandwidth, so giving 'studio quality' (unlike a telephone line, which restricts the frequency).

NAB: National Association of Broadcasters (US).

Nab centre: A circular device clipped into the centre of a tape spool, and fitted over the spindle of a tape recorder.

OB: Outside broadcast.

P as B (BBC): Programme As Broadcast.

P as R (BBC): Programme As Recorded.

Package (BBC): A broadcast report consisting of a journalist's voice plus at least one insert of actuality.

Pot point: A suitable moment, such as the end of a sentence, in which a piece of audio can be stopped early if required. (E.g.: This piece is 2 minutes, but there is a pot at 1′.12″.)

PPM: Peak programme meter. A device with scale and needle measuring sound levels. (More technically, the measurement of peak values of broadcast output.) (See also VU meter below).

Q & A (question and answer) (IR): *See* **Two way** (below).

Racks: The room in a radio station containing engineering equipment.

Remote studio: A small studio, usually unstaffed, connected to a main studio centre by landline or radio link.

ROT: Record Off Transmission. Literally, a recording of the broadcast signal via a radio tuner. Sometimes used (less accurately) to mean any recording of studio output.

Splicing: The process of cutting and rejoining tape for editing purposes.

Splicing tape: A specialized sticky tape designed for editing.

TBU: Telephone balancing unit. Equipment used to balance (or match) the studio output with an incoming telephone line for recording or live transmission.

Traffic: The department in an independent radio station which allocates commercials for transmission.

Trail (programme trail): A short item advertising a future programme.

Two way (BBC): A discussion or interview between studios remote from each other. Frequently used to mean a reporter questioned on air about their story. In commercial radio, this type of reporting is called a Q & A (question and answer).

Voice piece/voicer (BBC/IR): A news story explained by a reporter within a bulletin.

Vox pop (*vox populi*): Literally 'voice of the people'. A series of comments on a single issue gathered at random from members of the public and edited into a sequence.

VU meter: Volume Unit meter. A device to measure sound levels. It is less common in professional equipment than the PPM (*see* above), being more inaccurate at some frequencies.
Wrap (IR): *See* **Package**.

Index